the table.

an invitation to life at full capacity

d.d. white

Copyright 2024 © d.d. white

All rights reserved.

No part of this book may be reproduced, stored in a retrieval system, or transmitted by any means, electronic, mechanical, photocopying, recording, or otherwise, without written permission from the author.

ISBN (Paperback): 979-8-9917098-5-9
ISBN (eBook): 979-8-9917098-4-2

To Daisy, my dear flower:
creative, considerate, and courageous
&
to Jack, my warrior:
sincere, strong, and sweet.

May you both love to live and live to love.
May you always be seated at the table,
next to the King
who sees, knows, and loves you best.

This project represented doing a *hard thing*,
taking a risk.
Life is too short to worry about what
other people think.
Just do it. Do the *hard things*.

– Dad

contents

Preface vii

Prologue xi

The Table? 1

Part I. You are... 11

    You Are Seen 11

    You Are Chosen 29

    You Are Enough 41

    You Are Worthy 63

    You Are Adopted 87

    You Are Invited 111

Part II. Now what? 133

    You Eat 139

    You Connect 169

    You Share 193

    You Choose 213

Closing 235

preface

Jesus once said that He came to give life.
Life—more abundant, more rich, more beautiful.

>Stop.

>>Read that above line.
>>One more time.
>>Nice and slow.

This book is a plea to actually believe and live this promise out.

Now, before you judge this book, let me make this clear:

>**This is not a *prosperity gospel*.**

There will obviously be some challenges throughout our life. It was true for Jesus and His friends.

>It will be true for us too.

But let's not let the fear of prosperity rob us of a life we are promised.

> *The thief comes only to steal and kill and destroy; I came that they may have life, and have it abundantly.*
>
> –Jesus

No, this is not *a* prosperity gospel. This is *the* gospel.

Gospel simply means "good news."

If you are not interested in living this life to the fullest or actually believing ancient words in a book that many write off as fable, then I recommend putting this book down. It will be a waste of time. You won't get any extra credit from the words in front of you.

> But...
> if you have ever wondered
> If there was anything else to life,
>
> turn the page.

the table.

This is a book for those of us who are hungry.
Who know, deep down, that there is something more.

    If that's you, then open your mind and continue reading.

    But first:

        Father, Jesus, Holy Spirit –
        be with us.
          Guide us.

            We are here,
            and we expect
              You to lead.

prologue

My parents had a tiny plastic table with little plastic chairs. The top was a yellowish-white, and the legs were blue; a blue that only lived in the eighties.[1]

This is where I ate my fish sticks, my chicken nuggets, and my TV dinners. This is where I, daily, faced the battle of eating the vegetables. This plastic table is where I spent a good amount of time of my childhood, waiting for the food to go away or for my mom to give in. Many life lessons were learned at this plastic table with the name "Playskool" etched into the side. This is where I learned that if I secretly "dropped" my broccoli on the ground, it would look as if I had eaten it. And eating food—all of it—was a good thing to the big people in the house. I learned that this table was often the only thing between me and what was next: cartoons or continuing my imaginary game in the backyard. A house rule was that I could not leave the table until I was done with

---

[1] Along with big hair, rock and roll, and Alf.

my food, which I remember as being an eternity. This table is where I learned theater: acting like I was full or tired, or oftentimes the infamous *tummy ache*. This table is a kid's most dreaded obstacle when trying to get to the promised land. So, I would sit there and stare at my half-eaten meatloaf, thinking of ways to dispose of the green beans.

This, my friends, was the kid's table.

My eyes always drifted to the big table—the adult table. The glorious wooden table with fancy table legs and illustrious wooden engravings. To a kid, it was the green grass on the other side: the dream, the big leagues, the show. The food and the conversation always seemed better at that table. I sure thought it was, because it always felt like I was missing out.

The "good" food is at that table.
They have jokes at that table.

All the cool people were at that table.

And I wasn't.

They would laugh and cry and talk about… I don't know; I wasn't in the conversation. I just knew I was missing out. I wasn't at that table. I was at the kid's table—the cheap table. The plastic, little blue table.

the table.

    I was stuck—
        stuck at the kiddie table.
            Have you ever been there?[2]

One of these days, I would whisper under my french-fried breath. I used to believe that one day, I, little Davy, would join the ranks of the chosen ones and sit at that grown-up table.

    I wanted to sit there.
        I desired a seat at that table.

One day, feeling brave, I walked straight up to my dad and boldly declared, "I want to eat at the table; the big table, the wooden table… the good table."

He looked at my mother and pulled up a chair. He put a couple of phone books on it,

    and I sat.

I looked at my younger sister, who was now beneath me, and I smiled an *I made it* smile. As I sat there,

    I felt magnificent.
        I felt important.
           I felt cool.
                I felt like a somebody.
                      I had made it.

---

[2] I am not only talking about tables.

I was about to take my first esteemed bite.

    I reached for my fork, and my elbow tapped my glass. I spilled my milk.

        Back to the kiddie table I went.

        It would be months, maybe even years, before I earned my way back

                to the adult table.

* * *

Fortunately, this is not the life we live.

I believe we are invited to sit at *the table* as sons and daughters of God—the good table, the most beautiful table in the universe. You may be thinking, *Why would God worry about me sitting at the adult table?* Well, He's not; He's a lot more interested in a spiritual table. A symbolic table. A table that is better than the fancy, engraved table we lusted over as kids.

I am convinced we are invited to sit and dine with the king of kings, to eat from the glorious kitchen of heaven. I believe we have a seat, with our name on it, at this table—

        even when we spill the milk.

the table?

I believe somewhere out there, there is a table.
   A spiritual table. An invisible table. Let's call it God's table.

Before you count me as a lunatic and stop reading, imagine with me that there is such a table. It would symbolize blessing, honor, salvation, connection-all the good, spiritual things. Many would call it a spiritual destination or goal. But I want you to think of it not necessarily as a place to go when you die, but something available now. Something we can experience or get to here on Earth today. I want to present to you the idea that an abundant, full, best life is not only some sort of future happening—it is available now.

   Right now.
      For you
         and for me.

This is nothing new; this message has been told, taught, preached, written about, and talked about. However, this is a message to my generation, especially if you call yourself a Christian.[3]

I overheard some *Christian* folks talking one day; I heard them say, "We are waiting for eternity to live in light of eternity." If you are anything like me, you had to read that a few hundred times to depict the meaning, but in English, it means we often wait to die to finally live.[4] To experience *heaven* or some sort of *ideal life*, the common belief is that we must die first.

I was taught this as a child: that when someone dies, they're in a *"better place."* That one day—*not today*, but one day—we will have reached the goal. While there is truth to some of that, the message Jesus presents is quite different.

Yes, there is everlasting life promised after our life on Earth for those who believe, but Jesus was not only about the destination. He was about the journey as well.

journey > destination

or

journey < destination

How about

journey = destination?

---

[3] I have a friend named Christian. I am not talking about him.
[4] Sounds terrible to me.

The idea that only when we die will we finally experience the life we had dreamed of is not only tragic, but it is depressing. It is painful to think my whole life here on Earth is just the waiting room for what's next.[5]

Really? Just waiting?

No.

We are invited to live and experience that true, full, and beautiful life now.

For the sake of the illustration, let's pretend that this so-called life is a table—a privileged table we desire to sit at. In humanity, from the beginning of time, it has been a goal to sit at this invisible, theoretical, spiritual table. To experience a deeper life, an enlightened or awakened reality, here on Earth. Really, to experience something more: to go to the next level. In my experience, one of the few elements that nearly every culture, group, or religion shares is the idea that there is something more than our current reality.

There's got to be more out there.

You have felt it before, right? The feeling that this life can't be it. You wake up, go to work, come home, go to bed, and do the same thing all over again tomorrow. You thought the "more" was found in family or friends, the dream job, making a lot of money, or becoming famous.

But you didn't find it there.

---

[5] I once waited four hours for a ride at Disneyland. The ride was fun, but the wait was not worth it.

There are countless stories of people making it only to report that something is still missing once they get there.

I will never forget the time I was with a friend of mine who was on my university baseball team. After a night of fun, celebrating the spoils of a big win, he looked at me with a tear welling in his eye and said, "This is great, but I feel like I am missing something... there's gotta be something more—this can't be it." It may have been the late hour we were talking, it might have been the alcohol he consumed earlier that evening, or it could have even just been a weird moment, but I have come to realize that he was touching on an age-old question: Is there anything else? Is there more? Is this it?

This can't be it.

Some call it zen and some call it salvation, while others call it paradise, heaven, or nirvana. Some still call it an awakening, and some just call it woke.[6]

As a follower of Jesus, I want to challenge the thought that all of these ideas stem from a suggestion that we can be connected in a deeper way to something bigger in life and to its good things. In other words, there has to be a way to have a relationship or unique connection with something deeply spiritual.

This pursuit has been a goal for every people group, every tribe, and every tongue. There is no discrimination

---

[6] This word has been used a lot in many different ways. It's definitely the most stylish yet controversial word to call it.

when it comes to something more. My question to ponder: could that "something more" really be a reality?

So, what's this talk about a table? Tables are one of the most uniquely human places for dining and connection. Before there was the Internet, before there were cell phones, and before there was even TV, information and gatherings happened around tables: big tables, small tables, rectangular tables, and round tables; boardroom tables, poker tables, teacher tables, and snack tables. Tables have been around forever—from ancient Egypt to the times of the Greeks, Romans, and our everyday modern families. Good things happen around a table: like food, family, and friends. Tables are a big deal.

So imagine this "something more" as a spiritual table. If you symbolically sit at this table, you experience the "something more" we have been discussing. So here is the million-dollar question: How do we get there? How can we sit at this table? How can we connect deeper with the divine? This is the question that has caused wars and splits and persecutions and... belief.

In the ancient Hebrew scriptures,[7] there is this fascinating thought that the God of the Bible prepares a table for you. Again, imagine this spiritual table with me. In Psalm 23, David, the man famous for killing giants and being a dude after God's own heart, pens this line in a poem:

> *You prepare a table before me...*

---

[7] Just a fancy way of saying the Old Testament of the Holy Bible.

For whatever reason, the writer chose to use this vocabulary to describe his experience with the divine. Again, to convey his current experience on Earth with God. Notice the tense; it's not past tense or future tense, but present.

> Present tense.

Today, I want to urge you to believe.
Believe that there is such a table and there is such a life

> in the present tense.

This table we are discussing is waiting for you.
Waiting for you not to be perfect, but for you to simply come, reach for the chair, and sit. Some of the chairs at the table are dusty—waiting for people to simply sit.
So, what is the purpose of this writing you have found before you?

> To tell you to go. Go and sit.
>
> Time is wasting.

A great mentor of mine, John Maxwell,[8] once shared that how you spend your time is more important than how you spend money.

So, here's a question for you: how are you spending your time?

> Think about yesterday.
>
> Think about today.
>
> What are your plans for tomorrow?

---

[8] My mentor through books and video teachings. I have yet to meet him. I would love to one day!

the table.

Are you walking around life waiting for the next big thing? Waiting for the tides to change? Waiting for the right age? Waiting until you have everything figured out? Waiting for the planets to align? You might as well be waiting to die. I know it's harsh, but that's the reality for many of us. Waiting is often a waste of time. Don't spend your life waiting because, before you know it, the lights will fade and you will be looking at yourself in the mirror at the end of your life and think, *what did I even do?*

>Don't let that happen.
>
>Quit waiting.

Yet, here is the kicker. God is also waiting—
>waiting patiently but urgently for you
>>to join Him.
>>
>>To sit with Him at the table.
>>
>>To experience your best life.
>>
>>Today: right now.

Why else would David declare:

>*You anoint my head with oil;*
>*my cup overflows.*
>*Surely your goodness and love will follow me*
>*all the days of my life,*
>*and I will dwell in the house of the Lord forever.*[9]

He is not talking about life after death. He literally says "all the days of my life." My current, undead life.[10] The reality is

---

[9] Psalm 23:5-6.
[10] Thank God.

that we are invited to sit at that table today, not because of what we have done or not done, but because of who we are. You are invited because you are you.[11]

And that, my friends, is very good news.

***

Jesus used to teach in parables—which were little narratives meant to teach a lesson. Jesus was the ultimate storyteller. What a cool thing.

I adore stories.

May I share one? A parable?

A fun one that my students, kids, and buddies love.

The Parable of the Spoon

Long ago, there was an inventor. As he sat down to drink some soup one day, he grew tired of the soup getting into his mustache, for he drank it like a warm cup of coffee. He began to think of an apparatus that could carry the food to his mouth. Over the next few weeks, he began this new task to solve this petty situation. He looked around his house and found some leftover metals from past projects. The inventor then began to spin some ideas in his mind, designing and sculpting a spoon—the first of its kind. It was a beauty: stunning metals and grandiloquent engravings down the handle.

---

[11] I'll get into this more later.

Immediately after, the inventor gathered ingredients outside to make some stew, hoping to give this new spoon of his a try. While he walked amongst the grasses and dirt, the spoon slipped out of his pocket and tumbled into the soil. After collecting the ingredients, the inventor returned home, unaware that the spoon was missing.

Once the stew had been cooked, the inventor sat down to not only eat his stew but to try out his new invention he called a "spoon." But to his surprise, it was gone! He rushed outside to look for it but could not find it. Hungry, he returned to the table to eat without his spoon; he would construct another later.

Later that day, the spoon peeked up and looked around. The spoon began to wonder, *What am I supposed to be? What am I supposed to do?* The spoon looked around and saw grass and rocks. It also saw different garden tools near the shed, but what caught this little spoon's attention was the shovel leaning against the house. The spoon mused, "Well, I guess I kind of look like that," and then proceeded to dig tiny little holes all over the yard.

I know, I know—this tale is pretty far-fetched, but follow me here: Imagine this little lost spoon had been missing for a year or two, maybe even ten. It sat in the dirt, scooping hole after hole, feeling and believing that this was its destiny: to dig in the Earth. Nothing more, nothing less.

Pretty sad, eh? Have you ever felt bad for a spoon? Let's keep going.

Then, one day years later, the inventor, walking about, caught a flash from its rusted and dirt-stained handle. The inventor, curious, went to see what this flash was and found the spoon! Filthy, used, abused, and stuck in the mud.

Now, what does the inventor do, you ask?

Well, although the inventor went on to make other spoons, forks, and utensils in time, he went inside his kitchen with this spoon in hand. He gently washed the spoon in warm, soapy water. He polished it and cleaned it. He then sat down and enjoyed a bowl of soup using his first spoon. The spoon then realized—for this, it was made.

* * *

Yes, it's a silly story.

Yes, spoons don't have the brains to think and wonder.

Yes, I may have gone too far.

But...

I wonder how many of us right now are sitting in the dirt when we were designed to sit at the table.

The creator's table.

In other words, we can live our whole life working hard, performing, and doing what we *think* we should be doing. We chase purpose and abundant life, but it's all nonsense if we are not where we are supposed to be. As a matter of fact, it's all for nothing if we are not in the inventor's hands.

part one
you are...

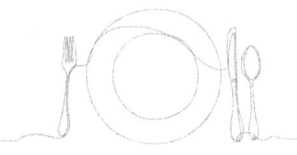

you are seen.

"It is a weekend retreat," my dad said, urging us to join. My wife and I looked at each other; early in our marriage and with our busy schedules as newfound teachers, we hesitated to say yes.[12] After some thought, we decided getting away for a weekend wouldn't be half bad. After all, it was a retreat. Little did I know, I was saying yes to an experience that would shape the rest of my life.

We thought we were getting away to relax by a fire and sip on some hot cocoa. We didn't realize it was actually a silent retreat focused on experiencing God. We found ourselves surrounded by folks of all ages and walks of life crammed into one cabin. Apparently, there was a structure and a timeline to the "retreat."[13]

---

[12] This was before kids, a mortgage, and keeping our heads on straight. We *thought* we were busy.

[13] Can kiss relaxation goodbye

The first night was led by a woman named Cathy, a semi-hippie musician with a remarkable ability to usher those around her into the presence of God.[14] In the first evening session, she asked a simple question:

"What are you longing for?"

While I was dreaming of hot cocoa and maybe a nice nap, Cathy invited all of us to participate. She asked us to speak *one* word about what we desired; she wanted to do this as a group.

The mood was set in a beautiful candlelit room. She softly played guitar, and a few began to speak out single words describing their heart's longings. I wasn't really paying attention when all of a sudden, a word bubbled up from my soul.

Without even thinking, I blurted out a word:

"Recognition."

When I realized what had happened, I was overwhelmed with embarrassment. As other *nobler*, more *Christian* words were spoken like "wisdom," "love," and "Jesus," there I sat uncomfortably because I had just revealed my deepest, maybe darkest, desire (which I didn't even know about). All I was thinking about was how everyone else in this cabin, including my wife and parents, must've had thoughts about me.

---

[14] Cathy Hardy. Beautiful soul. I am sure you can find her on that thing called the internet.

As I sat in anguish, I thought about all the words in my mental dictionary. I thought of the beautiful longings and desires I do have,[15] and was mortified that the only word I could think to say was that one.

Recognition?
What?!

How prideful and selfish I felt and looked! I could just feel all of the eyes looking at me and thinking, *Wow kid, what are you doing here? You know this is a Christian retreat? This cabin is for good people.*

I felt ashamed.

As I sat there pondering the word "recognition," I felt the need to lie down. As the evening progressed with some soaking, meditative music, I fell into a bit of a daydream-like state. It was a good time to start a conversation with myself and with God.

Do I really desire to be recognized?
Lord, what does this even mean?
Am I just prideful to the core?
What do other people think of me now?

As I was chewing on these thoughts, peace fell over me—a peace I cannot describe in writing.[16] I opened my eyes and found a book next to me. It was called *Invited*, by Lorie Martin. I opened it to a random page and read these words:

---

[15] Why couldn't I just say hot cocoa?
[16] I know it's starting to sound pretty outlandish, but hang in there.

> "You are invited to the table with Jesus Christ...
> this means that you are *recognized*,
> recognized as somebody,
> recognized as a person,
> you are wanted, and you are seen
> and accepted by the King."

I was blown away. I began to see a deeper and more symbolic meaning and definition of the word "recognized."

All of a sudden, I was not embarrassed.
That was my word.
My deep desire. My secret longing.
Joy welled up in my heart.

A picture came to my mind: Jesus was walking through a small crowd, and all of the people were out trying to get His attention. They wanted to touch Him; they wanted Him to heal them. In all of the commotion, Christ turns His gaze upon me. He looks at me.

The king of the universe looked at me.
He saw me.
He called out my name.
He recognized me.
And He said, "Come, sit with me. Be with me."

In my mind's eye, I was watching a spiritual movie where I was the star. From this image, I learned something revolutionary to me: in all of the commotion and busyness of the crowd, when it seems like you are just another average human, He looks at you. He doesn't see *a sinner saved by grace*—He sees a son. He sees a daughter. He sees someone of value, someone who is

> wanted,
> > desired,
> > > seen,
> > > > and recognized by the King.

Being involved in the public education system for over a decade, I've noticed that recognition is one of the deepest longings of every kid, as well as every human.

To simply be noticed.

There is nothing like public (or even private) recognition. In the classroom, I will often hold up someone's classwork and say, "Wow, I can really tell this student worked hard and did their best on this. This work is incredible!" You should see how these kids' faces light up when they hear that.

When I began my career in the classroom, I wasn't just there to teach reading and arithmetic; my goal was to create an incubator of strength: a wave of kids who were confident and knew they were uniquely valued. I started an end-of-the-week activity in my class called "Brag Time" to help with this. It's a moment when students can publicly brag or say something good about someone else in the room. Of course, I had a couple of rules:

> Firstly, you had to be specific (to keep kids from saying, "I brag on Kelly because she's cool").

Secondly, it had to be something you had seen or heard from the week—something impressive to them.

I also encouraged them to brag about someone they normally don't talk about or even hang out with. What transpired was magical.

I have seen students bring out the gold in others. I have seen the "unseen" or "invisible" students get bragged on, and it absolutely changes their behavior. I have seen the *cool* sixth graders break down and cry when they hear someone else say nice things about them. All of this simply because someone noticed something—they were seen, recognized, and called out on something good they thought no one saw.

Every kid wants to be seen. Scratch that: every *human* wants to be seen.[17] I still, as a middle-aged adult man, yell out to my wife to watch me when I feel like I'm doing something cool. Kind of like I did to my mom when I was learning to ride my bike. Just yesterday, I was riding scooters with my kids. I was bunny hopping from the street up the curb. My kids thought I was pretty cool, and I thought to myself, *It would be awesome if my wife saw me doing this.* So, I told my son to run inside to get Mommy to watch me.[18]

There is a human need to be seen: deep down inside, each of us desires to be noticed and recognized.

Deep down inside of you, you want to be seen.

---

[17] Many will go to great lengths to achieve this. Been there, done that.
[18] She wasn't impressed.

the table.

Have you ever been in a public place, and someone across the restaurant calls out your name to say *hi?* Everyone looks at you. Remember the feeling of pride? It comes from being recognized. How about when your supervisor pulled you aside privately and said, "*I see your hard work; you are doing a great job.*"

Recognition is key.

It can also be flipped.
    To be recognized for something negative.
        It's called shaming.

Have you ever been called out for something you weren't proud of? In some cultures, shaming is an incredibly effective way of government.[19] The research indicating its adverse effects on people is astoundingly bad, but it works.[20]

    It keeps people down.
    "*In their place,*" some might say.

        But that's not our gospel.
        Our place is where we are seated at the table.

Negative recognition is not what the table is about. Being invited to the table is like being requested to see the president.
        It is for honor.

---

[19] And, unfortunately, some families and classrooms.
[20] Works meaning in a not-so-good kind of way.

Honor is what we get to experience with the God of the scriptures. He is calling out your name. Check this out:

> But now thus says the Lord, he who created you: "Fear not, for I have redeemed you; I have called you by name, you are mine."[21]

Part of the human condition is the desire to be noticed. We were literally created with the desire to be recognized infused into our DNA.

And being called out *by name* in honorable recognition is part of the good news.

I remember that, growing up, I was never the most outgoing or most social. I would even be shy around my grandma and hide behind my mom and dad. I seemed to have a good amount of friends at my elementary school, but I will be honest, one nagging lie that I seemed to always believe all through my childhood and into my adult life was that I wasn't very significant. I wasn't cool enough, I wasn't funny enough, and I wasn't good enough. I was just a kid, not interesting enough for real conversation and not cool enough to be picked out in a crowd. I was the kid whom adults would joke about, saying, "We just can't get this kid to shut up…" Meaning: this little person does not talk. And I didn't. Not because I had nothing to say—believe me, I had plenty to say—but because I didn't feel like others wanted to

---

[21] Isaiah 43:1

hear what I had to say.[22] It wasn't worth being said. Have you ever been there?

One memory that sticks out in my mind was when a guy named Rex Hudler was speaking at a local event. He was a professional baseball player and a professional athlete, which in my mind was like the ultimate cool.[23]

He was to speak in front of hundreds of adults at some event that my parents dragged me to. We were sitting somewhere in the middle of the crowd, and I was wearing my little league jersey because we had just finished a game earlier in the day. I couldn't have been older than ten, but during this talk, he noticed me. He called on me and had me stand up. He used me in some illustration or point he was trying to make. The people clapped and cheered for me. I don't remember a word that was said, but I remember how I felt. Man, I felt like I had just won the lottery. I remember thinking it was such an honor and wondering why he would choose me. Out of all these people, hundreds of people, he picked little old me. Insignificant me. After the event, people noticed me. They recognized me as the *guy who stood up*. People said hi to me, they waved to me, and they smiled at me. It made me feel important.

This is a truth that I have found to be crucial in my faith. Not only am I saved by grace, as many of our Christian friends have written on their social media bio, but I am *recognized*.

---

[22] It's true, I wanted to talk about cartoons. But you get the point.
[23] He also had such a cool first name. I was awe-struck.

> I am recognized as a child of God.
>> I am wanted,
> and I am significant in the kingdom of God.
>> I am big. I am seen.
>>> And not just seen, but truly noticed.

Only...

Some of us are afraid to be seen. We are so absolutely certain that what the other person will see in us as insufficient in some fundamental way.

> We are afraid that if someone truly *sees* us,
>> we will not measure up to
>> their expectations of us.

Unfortunately, it's not just a few people who struggle with this. The majority of the world struggles with this. According to Dr. Joe Rubino, approximately 85% of people worldwide have issues with self-esteem. That's nearly nine out of every ten people you would come across in a day. Just so you know, I am raising my hand even as I type this.

And the world we get to live in has its own unique challenge: it's called social media.[24] We live in a comparison culture. When we scroll, we are filled with images of *perfect*

---

[24] Don't get me wrong; there are plenty of good things that come with social media, like staying connected with family or friends or innocently stalking others. Don't say you've never done it.

people on *perfect* vacations with the *perfect* dog. To say it's challenging is an understatement.

I am a shorter guy, which has not helped with my feelings of insignificance. Even though I have never really admitted it, being a small dude has hurt and even still bombards my self-confidence today.[25] I have done some leadership studies, and even in sociology, people tend to follow what attracts them. In our modern society, tall, muscular, and handsome guys are typical leaders, husbands, and men.

Even in biblical times, Israel asked Samuel for a king, and God chose Saul, who was "a head taller than everyone else." Take a look around. Look at the majority of CEOs of corporations—tall; look at most lead pastors of large churches—tall. Look at America's history of presidents: they all are very tall men, except for James Madison of course, who stood at a whopping five feet and four inches. A simple Google search shows the average height of American presidents is around six feet. The current average height of men in the United States is 5'9". So, for whatever reason, we are electing non-average guys to be our leaders. We have heard the term "privilege" used in many aspects before, but can I call out tall privilege?[26] I am halfway joking, but on a serious note, why do taller people have a better chance of climbing the corporate ladder than me and my height-challenged friends?[27] Maybe I am just whining, but I share this because it falls into my feeling of insignificance. Feelings

---

[25] Obviously, this isn't true for all the short people. Napoleon, anyone? Prince? Alvin?

[26] I don't dislike tall people; some of my best friends in the world are tall.

[27] I feel like I am whining. Am I whining?

of unimportance and the lack of the qualities of manhood and leadership are ingrained into the way I look. I am being vulnerable.

It may not be being short for you, but what is it?

Is it the way you talk? The way you walk? Maybe it's the breakup you went through or the job you have (or don't have).

What mental saboteurs flood your brain?

We are usually our own biggest critic.
Why do many of us live as our biggest shamer?

It is because we often listen to the wrong voices.

According to themes of the scripture, our invitation and recognition often come in the "still, small voice."[28] Not the loud, competing, busy voices.

Stop listening to the wrong voices.
But how do you know which one is right?
You will know when you hear it.

Let me say it this way: one day, I think I was about a sophomore in high school, a very pretty girl walked up to me. She looked me straight in the eye and said, "You look like a miniature model." I took this as a huge compliment. Even though it was a backhand way of saying I was short, she still said I looked like a model. That's a win.

When the winter formal came around, I devised this grandiose plan to ask this girl to the dance with me. After all, I

---

[28] According to Elijah. Check out 1 Kings 19:11-12.

looked like a model to her, right? I went to buy some balloons, and I tied a really, really long string to them. At the top, attached to the balloons, was a note: "I would be a mile high if you went to formal with me. Signed, David."

Not to be obvious, I had my sister take her the balloons as I watched from around the corner.[29] My sister handed her the balloons, and this girl slowly pulled them down with a confused look on her face. I saw her reading the note, and I was expecting a smile or a laugh, fantasizing about her looking around for me and shouting, "Yes! Of course, I will go! You are a model!" But I noticed as she read the note, her face contorted into a shape that I had never seen on this girl's face before, and she quickly walked away. She never even responded. But I noticed a few days later one of the star basketball players asked her to go, and she said yes. Now, both the girl and this guy were about two feet taller than me, so it made sense, but in my mind, I just wasn't tall enough to be recognized. It might have been social suicide for my beautiful friend. It might just have been that she had other plans or didn't "like-me like-me," but to me, I felt invisible.

Have you ever felt like that?

That feeling where you believe you are not qualified or good enough? That feeling of being overlooked? This is a widespread thought, especially in today's world. Being involved in the public school, I have seen firsthand kids coming in with zero confidence. And unfortunately, it's not just one or two students.

---

[29] I was also scared out of my mind.

Shirzad Chamine,[30] in his best-selling book *Positive Intelligence*, describes these voices in our heads as saboteurs. Most of us are not immune to self-sabotage. The saboteurs live in our heads, triggering anger, shame, guilt, and other negative emotions. Here are some types of saboteurs to help you recognize your own self-sabotaging thoughts:

>Judge
>>Controller
>>>Hyper-achiever
>>>>Stickler
>>>>>Pleaser
>>>>>>Avoider
>>>>>>>Victim

Do any of those click with you? We are often at war with many of them at once. They love to work together. They often sound like:

>*You're not smart enough, or not athletic enough.*
>>*Not young enough, or not old enough.*
>>>*Not hip enough, or not fancy enough.*
>>>>*Not tall enough, or not strong enough.*
>>>>>*Not beautiful enough, or not doing enough.*

---

[30] Shirzad Chamine is the chairman of the largest coach-training organization in the world. He has trained the coaches and managers in most Fortune 500 companies as well as faculty at Stanford and Yale business schools.

... you're just not enough.
And they often take our voices to translate that all to
I'm not enough.

Part of the mission of this book is to prove yourself wrong. To prove that you are enough. You are more than enough. You are enough to be deeply seen by the King. The God of gods. The Lord of lords. The creator.
Really, the only One that matters.

The Bible is laced with people unseen by the world but seen by God.
Here are just a couple of fun examples:

- A simple shepherd. He was a boy, nothing more than the youngest of his family. He was not the tallest, the best-looking, or the strongest among boys, but he became the most powerful man in the land. He went from unseen to seen.

     Who am I? David.

- A young Jewish woman with no status, nothing to her name, becomes a central figure in Jesus' story. Scholars say she was nothing more than a young teenage girl. In antiquity, these types of people were not seen as much. Yet, God saw her.

     Who am I? Mary.

- A woman from a different culture. She was divorced multiple times, and would have been seen not only as an outsider but as dirty and shameful. Invisible to the world, but not to God. She would soon become the reason an entire town came to know Jesus.

Who am I? The woman at the well.

- A man known for his selfishness and greed, hated and ignored by nearly everyone. He often wouldn't be invited places or even seen with others. He was an outcast—until Jesus saw him.

Who am I? Zacchaeus

I could keep going, but I won't.

None of these people would have ever been voted the "most likely to succeed" in high school. These people are the ones we walk right by in the mall and do not even notice. But for whatever reason, God noticed them. He saw them, and it had nothing to do with their looks, their family, or their success.

Oh, wait. I have one more example.

- A person who is doing their best. They often struggle with a variety of issues, but they are still going. Sometimes, they deal with personal saboteurs about self-worth, personal values, and even their roles in life. They don't know it yet, but they are a significant piece of the puzzle for God's advancement of His kingdom in their family, their friends, their city, and their workplace.

Who am I? You.

the table.

God notices you.
    You are seen.
        Even right now.

Think about that. As you are reading these lines, you are being watched. Not in a creepy way, but in a loving, proud, fatherly way. The kind of watched that sees the beautiful potential in you.

                His eyes are on you.

---

table talk

Close your eyes and picture the King of kings sitting on a mighty throne. You are there, in the throne room, alone with God. You look at His face, and he looks at you. But as you look closer, you see that He is smiling. He is smiling directly at you..
    Stay there for as long as you need.

        What emotions or feelings did you experience?

           What might He say to you?

you are chosen.

Young in my teaching career, the school I was working at was putting on this event called "Donuts with Dad."[31] A few days before the event, I was encouraging the students in my class to go. I was hyping it up because if we had a good percentage of students go, the teachers would be given some sort of reward. There was a competition among teachers about who could send the most kids, and I was and am always up for competition. So I am selling it, and I am pretty good at that. There was this girl in my class... Let's call her Destiny.

Destiny was one of those kids that grew up a lot faster than her peers. By the time she was in sixth grade, she had already experienced things that no parent wants for their child: a rough home, rough friends, and rough school life; she was on a path to nowhere quick. She was also the biggest, baddest girl in the school—a foot taller than everyone else. Let's just say that there were many children who were afraid of her. Even some of the high schoolers would back down when this sixth grader stood up. Destiny was in one

---

[31] This was before it was "politically incorrect."

of my classes, and she and I had our own ups and downs, but at the end of the day, she was different with me. She, for whatever God-given reason, liked me, which was rare among the adults. As Donuts with Dad approached, I did my best to keep talking about it.

        Destiny did not have a dad.

Well, I guess you could say that she didn't have a dad in the picture. He was in and out of jail, on and off drugs, and on and off the streets. She couldn't remember the last time she spoke with him.

        But let's be clear: she did not have a dad.

I remember handing out flyers right before lunch. As I dismissed the students to leave that day, Destiny stayed seated in her chair. I was working on some lesson plans for the next class, not realizing she was still there until she grudgingly walked over to my table.

As I looked up, I noticed a shy, nervous Destiny, not the rough and tough girl I was used to dealing with. She was holding the Donuts with Dad flyer in her hand, and her head was hanging low. I glanced up and said, "Hey, Destiny, are you planning to get some lunch? Do you have any questions?" She sat down at my table. Trying to figure out what to do or say, I stared at her. She looked up at me with a little water in her eyes; I understood. I stood up and said, "Hey, you know what? I like donuts, and I really like you. I would love to go grab a maple bar with you. You in?" Then jokingly added, "You're pretty much my adopted daughter, right?"

Destiny lit up.

She was still trying to act like the tough girl she portrayed, but I saw a glimmer that affected me to the core. A sparkle in her eye that spoke a billion words for her. She said, "I like donuts, too," and nodded her head.

As she walked out of the room the day, she walked with a bit of pep in her step. Just as she was in the threshold of the classroom door, she turned and said, "Can I... ask you something?" There was a nervousness in her voice.

"Can I call you Papa?"

I immediately broke into a massive smile, and I said, "Absolutely!" Then as she ran off to lunch, she looked back and said, "Love ya, Papa!"

We went to Donuts with Dad the next morning. She showed up on time (which was hardly the case any other day), and it seemed as if she was dressed up just a little bit more than usual.

The donuts tasted extra good that day.[32]

As the year went by, she developed a sweet trust with me, and we got to the point where she would often eat lunch in my classroom at my table and talk to me like I was her papa. A handful of her followers frequently joined us. As we grew in our friendship, she asked me why I was the way I was. She had never met a teacher or even a man like me. I shared that I followed Jesus and his teachings.

She smiled.

---

[32] They are good any day, really. Donuts are my kryptonite. I could never pass up a maple bar or French cruller. But this day was much different.

She then joked, "Could you pray for me? Because boy, do I need it." Later that day, I gathered a few other teachers, and we prayed.

The last few months of that school year were beautiful. She had such an influence with the students that I had the best-behaved class on the block. She made sure everyone was paying attention and being respectful. She also led a whole group of my class to Jesus.

The last day of school was her birthday, and I'll never forget what happened as she left for summer that day. She turned and gave me a hug and said, "Thank you, Papa. Thanks for choosing me."

What was meant as a day of gift receiving for the birthday girl ended with her giving me the gift instead.

She said it was the best year of her life.

That's why our God created donuts.[33]

***

Blessed is the God and Father of our Lord Jesus Christ. For he has chosen us, before the foundations of the world to be holy and blameless before him.[34]

Did you catch that?

Before the foundation of the world was laid,

you were *chosen*.

Yes, you.

---

[33] And because He is a good, good Father.
[34] Ephesians 1:3 and 4. One of my favorites.

The foundation is the very first thing done when building a house. You can't start building anything unless the foundation is in place.[35]

You were chosen *before* that.

> Let that sink in for a moment.

Our God is a God of choice. One of the best parts about this whole book is this: we have been *chosen* by the King of kings.

> *Chosen* to take a seat at His table.

Imagine with me a line of people ranging from all nationalities and all parts of history—every person who ever lived and ever will live. Imagine we are all on the playground, lined up against the chain-linked fence and picking teams. Jesus is a team captain. As He surveys the line looking for the person He wants to choose, His eyes fall upon you.

> And He says,
>> "You. You are who I want,"
>> and he calls you out
>> by name.
>
>> He chooses you.[36]

You have been chosen by God.
> You have been chosen to sit at the table.

---

[35] Actually, the water and sewer pipes go in before the foundation. I would imagine that God chose you even before the pipes.

[36] Chosen first—the ultimate respect on the playground.

But just because we've been chosen doesn't mean it's over.

You see, you have a choice too.

The ball is in your court.
Did you leave the chain link fence to walk to your side?
Did you find yourself walking to the wrong team?
Or, perhaps, are you stuck?
Stuck on the fence.

***

All throughout these ancient scriptures, God gives choices to His people.

I've always wondered why, in the Garden of Eden, God has the Tree of Good and Evil. Like, why not just have only the good trees for them? Make it easy?[37]

> *The LORD God made all kinds of trees grow out of the ground—trees that were pleasing to the eye and good for food. In the middle of the garden were the tree of life and the tree of the knowledge of good and evil.*[38]

It's not hidden or even off to the side—it's in the middle. God literally puts it where they will be passing it and seeing it all the time. He says to eat anything they want except for that one tree, the one in the middle.

The choice was theirs.

---

[37] It's like dangling a donut at the salad bar.
[38] Genesis 2:9.

The theme of *choice* is threaded throughout scripture.

- God gives Joshua a choice of who to serve. It would have been easier to follow the god of the land.

- Daniel has the choice to conform to the Babylonian world or stay true to what he believed. He could've had his fill of the best food around, but no.

- Joseph didn't have to stay with Mary; walking away would have been a simpler, less controversial option.

- John the Baptist didn't have to baptize Jesus. It might have saved his life if he didn't.

- Peter and the disciples had to choose to follow Him. Most believed they were out of their mind.

Jesus takes time in the middle of one of his most famous teachings to speak of two roads: one small and narrow, and one open wide. Choice is rampant in our lives, and especially in the lives of those who decide to follow Jesus. It all comes back to you: Your choice. One of the most beautiful things about the whole free will theology is that God had a choice to love us, and we, in return, have a choice to love, believe, and follow Him.

I have two beautiful kids.[39]

    Daisy and Jack.

        ***

---

[39] Warning: I am about to get sappy.

I didn't think I could love like I love them. There is something unique about a father's love. They did nothing to earn my love because it started before they did anything. It started before they had a choice to love me.

But you know what, even if they decided one day not to love me, it would never change the way I feel about them.[40]

In the same way, our Father loved us before we could even know how to love Him. In the church circle, you may have heard the phrase "while we were still sinners," which means even when we did not choose God, He loved us. Humans were the ones who beat Jesus, put the crown of thorns around His head, and hung Him on the cross. You and I were not there when that happened, but there are times in our lives when we mess up almost as badly. We sin.

The word "sin" is an ancient word that simply means "missed the target." It was often used in reference to archery, like when an archer shoots an arrow and doesn't hit the target. But nowadays, it seems it is only used by people in the church.[41]

> But the truth is that Jesus died for the sins or misses of *all* people.
> Even you.

So that time you lied, or lusted, or had those terrible thoughts—that day on the cross, Jesus saw them and chose you anyway.

---

[40] Can I just say, "Kids, I command you to love me and do everything I say for the rest of your life"? Actually, as I type that out, it sounds pretty creepy. No, it's better if they have a choice.
[41] Imagine a teacher telling a student after missing a question, "Sorry, bud, you sinned."

He looked upon you and said, "Forgive them, for they know not what they do."[42]

Why? Because we are His kids! We are the *chosen* sons and daughters of God. He shows great love, but also great patience. Patience for you and your response.

I often marvel at how much I love my kids, even when they throw their fits or write on the wall. If I had every kid in the world lined up and I could choose any of them to have, I would, without a doubt, choose Daisy and Jack. I don't care how messed up they are—to me, they are perfect. They always will be. Why? Because I know them. I was there the day they were born and I have watched them grow. There is nothing that could ever take the place of my two children.

In the same way, God was there when you were made. He watched you grow, and nothing can change the love He has for you. God still chooses you despite yesterday and even despite tomorrow. He knows what you have done, and He knows what you will do. He picks you still.

Know this: Whether you choose Him or not, He will always choose you.

Jesus once said

"You didn't choose me. I chose you..."[43]

to love and to sit at my table.

You are chosen.

---

[42] Luke 23:24.
[43] John 15:16.

Jesus' communication style focused on two things: He told great stories and asked great questions. The first four books of the New Testament have Jesus asking three hundred and thirty-nine questions. Although, when he asked people to follow him, it wasn't in question form.

> As Jesus was walking beside the Sea of Galilee, he saw two brothers, Simon called Peter, and his brother Andrew. They were casting a net into the lake, for they were fishermen. "Come, follow me, Jesus said, and I will make you fishers of men." At once they left their nets and followed him.[44]

Jesus said "follow me" thirteen times in the Gospels. He used these two simple words to call Peter, Andrew, James, and John as his disciples.

So, I wonder if the invitation to the table is more like: "Come, <u>sit at my table</u>."

Hmm, sounds about right.

---

[44] Matthew 4:18-20.

table talk

Read Ephesians 1:3–14.
Read it twice, slowly and intentionally.

Meditate on its words.
Let your meditation lead you to prayer, thanksgiving, and confession.

You were chosen first. Who or what do you need to choose? What decisions are you faced with today?

you are enough.

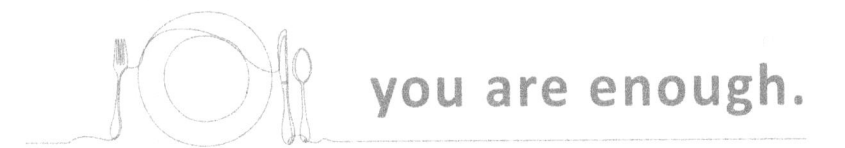

The chapter title is misleading,
because, actually, you are not enough.
What a bummer way to start a new chapter.[45]
But the truth is, left to our own, we don't measure up.
We will always lack.

But at the table, you are more than enough.

Again, from Psalm 23:
> *You prepare a table before me*
> > *in the presence of my enemies.*
> *You anoint my head with oil;*
> > *my cup overflows.*

When you are sitting at the table with God,
your cup overflows.

---

[45] Confused?

As I am writing this, I am visiting San Francisco. Along with the beauty of the city and its beautiful activities, there are plenty of homeless people. I was walking the streets of the city completely amazed at the disparity of finance. On the one hand, this location harbors some of the wealthiest people in the world. There are high rises towering into the fog, filled with top-tier people. On the other hand, it also holds tents and make-shift shelters in the alley with people who've hit rock bottom.

I was walking with my kids, and there was a young man sitting against the wall. As we walked by, he held out a large, empty styrofoam cup. Wrapped in a blanket, dirty and unshaven, he says, "Would you fill my cup? I've got nothing."

Again...

> *You anoint my head with oil;*
> *my cup overflows.*

When we are with God, we are more than enough.

The Parable of the Log

A young boy and his father were walking a trail in the forest one day when they came to a part of the trail with a fallen tree blocking the way. The boy looked at his father and asked, "Do you think I can move this tree out of our path?" The father replied, "Of course, you can—if you give it all you got."

> The boy put his bag down, got up against the log, and pushed.
>
> Nothing.

The boy stepped back, took a deep breath, stepped up again, and pushed.

Nothing. The log didn't even budge.

The boy stepped back again, this time stretching his arms a bit more and taking another couple of deep breaths. This time, he ran at the log with a fierceness the boy never knew he had. He connected with the log like a linebacker, with a mighty and powerful force.

Still, the log didn't move. Not even close.

The boy sat there in disappointment; he looked at his father and said, "You said I could move it! I gave it all I had, and I can't do it!" The father tenderly looked at his son and said, "I said you could do it if you gave it *all* you had."

"Dad, I did! I gave it my all! I couldn't move it if I tried for another 10 hours. I gave it all I had!"

Again, the father looked at his son with a smile, "But I am with you, and I am yours. You never asked me for my help. Let's do it together."

They walked to the log together, they pushed together, and the log rolled out of the path.

***

We are enough only when we tap into the presence of the Father.

When we sit at the table, our cup overflows.

> Left to our own devices, our cup is empty,
> and we resort to our human
> strategies to measure up.

The truth is:
> We all want to be full.

***

> We all want to make the grade.
> We all want to be enough.

So, how do we measure that?
We will often compare ourselves with everyone around us.

We live in a compare-and-contrast world. Comparing and contrasting is a skill I teach my students when we dissect a text,
a video, a picture, or an object. You may recall the good old-fashioned Venn diagram in school: the two circles that overlap in the middle.[46] How many of us learned that technique in third grade and have applied it to every area of our lives? We live in a society that is built on social Venn diagrams.[47]

> Can you relate?

> "Oh, Billy looks so healthy and in shape; I just
> can't seem to stick with it, and it shows."

---

[46] Let the flashbacks begin!
[47] Can you imagine the pile of worksheets?

"Oh, Sally just bought that hot new car; she's good with her finances, and I am living paycheck to paycheck."

"Oh, Jimmy has such good friendships; he's charismatic, and I am not. I can barely count any real friends I have."

"Oh, their marriage is perfect; they are always happy and traveling. My marriage needs and takes work."

"Oh, Jackie got the job because she's smart, and I am lacking."

"Oh, Bobby's kids play three sports, do music lessons, have straight A's, and are so well behaved. Mine—well, mine aren't doing that."

Blah, blah, blah, blah.[48]

This person is this, and I am not.

or

This person has that, and I don't.

They are like silent bullets being shot at us in every direction.[49] While most of us don't or wouldn't say these phrases out loud, they live quietly in our heads. Like an illness that we don't know about, slowly but surely doing everything it can to kill us.

The media seems to be pushing a certain look, and when we look into the mirror, we just don't measure up. Schools are forcing a certain type of student, and when we look at our

---

[48] I can keep going, but I will spare us the time and agony.
[49] Like a crazy Tarantino movie.

grades or kids, they don't compare. Our boss is projecting the perfect employee, and we cannot measure up. The church is preaching a flawless type of Christian, and we are not Christian enough.

The idea of being content with who we are and how we have been created is lost. We are now very good at looking in the mirror and being dissatisfied. Here are some signs that you might be stuck in the compare-and-contrast world:

- You don't get rid of negativity in your life.
- You're not determined to finish things.
- You find yourself addicted to scrolling through social media.
- You exaggerate a lot.
- When someone gets recognized or praised, you're a little bit jealous.
- You stay stuck in toxic situations (relationships/jobs/mindsets).
- You often doubt yourself (maybe even under the faux mask of humility).
- You struggle to make decisions.
- You struggle to live out dreams or achieve goals.
- You are depressed.

This is a short list of some (but not all) "stuck" characteristics that live among us. As you know, I have struggled with feeling good enough or qualified enough myself. But it's not just me. The entire human race—we have all toiled with it.

And we still do.

Usually, when someone is in this mindset of not being enough, they have one of two reactions: fight or flight. These terms are often used in regard to the human response to trauma or anxiety, yet they also seem to fit this context.

Let me explain.

Flight: Sometimes, when people feel they are not enough, they simply quit. They give up on themselves and they run away from it all. They fall into apathy, leading to depression, doom-scrolling, low energy, drugs, alcohol, and addiction. These people live a very empty life. I'm not trying to be mean; I am just being real because I have been there. No dreams, no hope, just the next stop. It's like a man getting free rides on a train headed nowhere.

Just leaving his life in the last town.

I believe David the Psalmist dealt with this and wrote directly to the fliers as he recalled:

> *My spirit grows faint within me;*
> > *my heart within me is dismayed.*
> *Answer me, Lord;*
> > *my spirit fails.*
> *Do not hide your face from me,*
> > *or I will be like those who go down to the pit.*[50]

The flier will often find themselves in "the pit." Whether "the pit" is mental, spiritual, or physical, these fliers run from the mental attacks and hide, thinking they are safe, but end up in an even worse position than before.

---

[50] Psalm 143:4-7.

But David realized something: If you will hide, hide in the Lord.

> *Rescue me from my enemies, Lord,
> for I hide myself in you.*[51]

There was a time in my life when the dreams and goals I had were to just get through the day. Let's bring this story full circle: My very first attempts at writing a book were terrible—absolutely terrible. I never thought or believed I could do it. As a student, I never liked or was any good (in my mind) at writing. As a matter of fact, in college, I was asked to write an article for a digital magazine published in Canada. I tried everything I possibly could to get someone else to write it. The project was a hassle because I never believed I was a good writer. I didn't do it. It never happened. I would read other articles or books and say to myself, "There is no way I could do something like that." So, what did I do? I just moved on. I quit. I didn't write. Even writing this book took me a very long time and a whole lot of mental willpower to do. And it took even longer in publishing! Not because I didn't have anything to say or because it wasn't ready, but because I wasn't willing.[52] It was much easier mentally to just hide. It took a lot of willpower because I didn't think I or it would ever amount to anything. It's hard to be determined if you feel there will be a sure failure.

One of the results of the compare-and-contrast world is fliers. We do it to cope. We do it to feel safe, but we end up

---

[51] Psalm 143:9.
[52] And scared… very scared.

just being quitters.[53] These fliers surround us more than you know. Friends, family members, colleagues, and strangers all around you have quit dreams in the name of safety.

> Maybe you relate? Maybe you have been there. Maybe you've quit something. Maybe you are in the midst of leaving. Perhaps you're running, avoiding, hiding. Maybe you're in the pit.[54]

> If you're going to hide, hide in the Lord, not the pit.

The other response to not feeling good enough is to fight.

The fighters go to battle with this mindset of exaggeration and lies. They usually exaggerate a bit and make themselves out to be someone or something they are not. These are the people whose profile pictures are doctored with filters to make them look like models. Their online biography says they are tall, tan, and handsome, but they are actually 5'3" and a little overweight. These are the mask wearers, the keyboard warriors, and the pufferfish of the world.

When threatened, a pufferfish puffs its body up with air and water to make itself look bigger, stronger, and fiercer to ward off conflict. When it is safe, it goes back to being its little

---

[53] I had a friend once tell me, "Quitters are losers and losers are quitters. You're not a loser and you're not a quitter." People pay big bucks for some hard truth sometimes.

[54] Not an armpit; the pit from the Psalm on the previous page.

old self. Do you know any human pufferfish? You may have been or may be one.[55] It is another response for protection, but again, to fight the feeling, we pretend. Then, at the end of the day, these people look in the mirror and are empty.

You might be thinking, *D.D., you are being a little hard on these people*. I am, because I have been there. The root of this problem stems from feeling inadequate. Fighting the insecure feelings is a strategy to cope. When people pretend to be someone they are not, they fight with fakeness. The fight is a lie.

Growing up, I was a big sports fan. I enjoyed all the usual American sports, like baseball, football, and occasionally basketball. I remember meeting some of the cool kids on my college campus.[56] In my mind, they were so cool, and I wanted to be their friend really bad.[57] One day, we were chatting it up and our conversation turned to sports, and I found out they were both avid hockey fans. Wanting to impress these newly added friends, I acted like I loved and knew all about hockey. This is the true definition of a poser. A fake.[58]

The conversation soon came to, "What team do you like?" At that point, to not be found out, I blurted out the only team I knew of: The Mighty Ducks. My answer was inspired

---

[55] I know I have been one heck of a puffer fish.

[56] Cool: a classic descriptive word that has never and will never go out of style.

[57] Why people are cool is all about perspective. These guys were cool mainly based on their trendy hairstyles and dress, which, frequently, is the first step to being cool.

[58] All of a sudden, I am embarrassed. Please don't judge—you've done it before too.

the table.

by the movie that every 80s and 90s baby grew up with and pretended to be a part of when they played street hockey.

And guess what? It worked. It got me by. They believed me. I sold it so hard that they truly thought I was an avid hockey and Ducks fan.[59]

The more I spoke to these friends, the more they would bring up hockey and The Mighty Ducks. Saying things like, "Did you see the game last night?" or "So and so is on fire right now."
    So, I did what any pufferfish man does in that position:
        I pretended and pretended and pretended.
            And I lied and I lied and I lied.

They were even buying me Mighty Duck paraphernalia because I portrayed myself to be a huge hockey and Mighty Duck fan.

The fight to fit in continued. I was in this fight because I was fighting the mindset that I wasn't cool enough to be their friend. This is what fighters do.

    It went on and on until one day, my friends invited me to watch the Stanley Cup (which is like the Super Bowl of hockey) with them. It was the year's biggest game, so I said yes, I'd watch the game with my new friends. I wore all of my Mighty Duck apparel. I Googled who was playing, and it wasn't the ducks, but I showed up looking like the ultimate hockey fan anyway. We ordered our food and did what guys do: engaged in small talk and manly yelling when something

---

[59] You can probably guess this isn't going to end well.

good happened on the TV that took up the whole wall. We were rooting for one of the teams, getting into the game, and quite frankly, I had no idea what was going on. I was just yelling when other guys were yelling. When they said it was a bad call, I agreed. When they said it was a good call, I agreed. It was a very weird experience.[60]

Now, in hockey, a key piece of knowledge to have is that they only play three periods.[61] This is something I didn't know; I assumed it was four quarters just like almost every other sport. I remember it came to the close of the third period, and the team we were cheering for (to this day, I still have no idea who that team was) was down by one point/goal/run (whatever they call it). We were closing in on the last period of the game and I blurted out, "Alright, men, in the next quarter, we are really going to have to pick it up! Here we go!"

The restaurant fell quiet.

People looked at me.

The guys looked at me.

All eyes

were on me.

You know that feeling when others are looking at you and trying to figure out if you are serious? That was one of those moments. I didn't know what else to do, so I kept saying stuff about the fourth quarter. It was at that instant I was found out. I had lived a double life, and my friends knew it. I was

---

[60] And pretty sad to say out loud.
[61] Basketball, football... you know, real American sports. Baseball is just weird. How did they come up with nine?

pretending to be someone I wasn't. I was fighting the "not good enough" feeling, and it finally came to the light.

> Embarrassing.
>
> The pufferfish finally got deflated.
>
> I fought the feeling of inadequacy, not with swords and armor, but with lies and pretending.

***

I think there is something to this note that Paul writes to Timothy:

> *But you, man of God, flee from all this, and pursue righteousness, godliness, faith, love, endurance and gentleness. Fight the good fight of the faith. Take hold of the eternal life to which you were called.*[62]

Timothy was a young leader in the church. I am willing to make a bet that good ol' Timmy struggled with his self-esteem every now and then. I am under the impression that Tim also tried to be a pufferfish sometimes. But his mentor, Paul, didn't let him stay there. In modern days, it could have possibly been written like this:

---

[62] 1 Timothy 6:11-12.

> *Hey Tim, quit all of the flying and fighting. Go after being who you truly are. If you are going to fight, fight with the Lord. You have already been chosen,*
>
> *so stand up and be yourself.*

Feeling inadequate is part of the human condition.
                                       Timothy is no exception.

          Some of us struggle with the idea of whether we have what it takes to be enough or not.

                                       You are not the only one.

I have flown away, and I have also tried to fight it out,
        but neither of these options free me from the feeling.
                To fly or to fight does not free anyone.

    This is not new. This is not a modern-day fault. This has been a common thread in humanity. From the beginning of time, societies have dealt with fitting in and measuring up.

    There was once this girl named Eve. One day, she was walking by a tree when a serpent told her that if she ate the fruit from the tree, she would be better—more like God. It was pretty much saying: "You can't be happy with your current self. Who you are right now isn't good enough."

The first sins ever committed on Earth stemmed from the feeling of not being good enough. The first lies from the devil targeted humanity's confidence.

How many of us have fallen victim to the lies?

How many of us have found ourselves flying or fighting?

***

There is this scene in the Bible that sticks out to me. It involves a couple of unqualified, not-good-enough guys doing something incredible.

There was this one guy named Peter. Peter, throughout scripture, gets this reputation of being a hard-core, no-nonsense follower of Jesus. Yet, this guy was actually just a fisherman and a failure.

In ancient times, a fisherman would have been similar to a worker at McDonald's today. There is nothing wrong with that, and I am not trying to be mean, I'm just using societal standards. I grew up being told, "If you don't do your homework, you will end up working at McDonalds."[63] But that was what these men were—just fisherman. They had no special schooling, no degree, and no advanced skill sets— just a menial job.

Peter and a bunch of other nobodies ended up following Jesus throughout his life. They witnessed miracles, teachings, and the life of God. After Jesus died, he left his followers with a command to go into the world and continue His work.

So, they do.

This ordinary guy, Peter, finds himself leading large-scale movements in the ancient world. He finds himself doing the things Jesus did, like miracles and teaching crowds.

---

[63] By the way, McDonald's has the best fries and coffee.

There is this fascinating scene that speaks to being enough. Peter and his buddy John had just healed a man who couldn't walk and led 5,000 people to Jesus. For this, they were arrested and questioned by the leading religious leaders of the day. And these guys, who by societal standards were not good enough, did this:

> *They had Peter and John brought before them and began to question them: "By what power or what name did you do this?"*
>
> *Then Peter, filled with the Holy Spirit, said to them:*
>
> *"Rulers and elders of the people!"*[64]

He goes into preach mode:

> *"If we are being called to account today for an act of kindness shown to a man who was lame and are being asked how he was healed, then know this, you and all the people of Israel: It is by the name of Jesus Christ of Nazareth, whom you crucified but whom God raised from the dead, that this man stands before you healed. Jesus is the stone you builders rejected, which has become the cornerstone. Salvation is found in no one else,*

---

[64] Acts 4:7-8.

> *for there is no other name under heaven given to mankind by which we must be saved."*[65]

But this is my favorite part:

> *When they saw the courage of Peter and John and realized that they were unschooled, ordinary men, they were astonished, and they took note that these men had been with Jesus.*[66]

So here are a couple of guys:
>> unschooled,
>> ordinary,
>> uncommon,
>> inadequate,
>> unqualified,
>> not good enough guys.

They don't fly or fight.

> They hide in the Lord and fight the good fight,[67]
>> and they do something incredible.

This is the same Peter that was just a fisherman. The same guy who, a little earlier in his life, messed up bad and denied Jesus three times.
> Talk about being unqualified.
> Talk about not good enough.

---

[65] Acts 4:9-12.

[66] Acts 4:13.

[67] Not trying to be contradictory. There is such a thing as a good fight. See 1 Timothy 6:12.

In the kingdom of the world, they were uneducated, illiterate, idiotic, ordinary, unqualified nobodies. But in the kingdom of God, they were *huge*.

The passage says that they spoke eloquently and were noted to have been with Jesus. Interestingly, according to these men who questioned them, significance and brilliance were associated with being with Jesus. To bring home this point, Jesus not only sees and recognizes you, but He qualifies you.

God doesn't call the qualified, but He qualifies the called.[68]

I know that I have struggled with self-image. I have fought and I have flown from the disease. But once I stopped relying on myself and started relying on God and who He said I was, I began to experience and do incredible things in my life.

Just as Jesus said I would.

> *Very truly I tell you, whoever believes in me will do the works I have been doing, and they will do even greater things than these.*[69]

My friend, you are not enough by yourself.
But with Jesus, you are more than enough. You are overflowing with "enough."
Have you discovered who you truly are and what your life in Christ is meant to be? This list of 30 truths reveal who God created you to be and how He wants you to live:

---

[68] This has been one of my mantras.
[69] John 14:12.

- I am complete in Him Who is the head over all rule and authority—of every heavenly and earthly power (Colossians 2:10).
- I am far from oppression and will not live in fear (Isaiah 54:14).
- I am born of God, and the evil one cannot touch me (1 John 5:18).
- I am holy and blameless before Him (Ephesians 1:4; 1 Peter 1:16).
- I have the mind of Christ (1 Corinthians 2:16; Philippians 2:5).
- The Spirit of God, who is greater than any enemy in the world, lives in me (1 John 4:4).
- I have received the Spirit of wisdom and revelation in the knowledge of Jesus (Ephesians 1:17-18).
- I have received the power of the Holy Spirit, and He can do miraculous things through me. I have authority and power over the enemy in this world (Mark 16:17-18; Luke 10:17-19).
- God supplies all my needs according to His riches in glory in Christ Jesus (Philippians 4:19).
- In all circumstances, I live by faith in God and extinguish all of the enemy's attacks (Ephesians 6:16).
- I can do whatever I need through Christ Jesus, who strengthens me (Philippians 4:13).
- God chooses me so I can proclaim the excellence and greatness of who He is (1 Peter 2:9).
- I am born again—spiritually transformed, renewed, and set apart for God's purpose—through the living and everlasting word of God (1 Peter 1:23).

- I am God's masterpiece, created to do good works that He has prepared me to do (Ephesians 2:10).
- I am a new creation in Christ (2 Corinthians 5:17).
- In Christ, I am dead to sin—my relationship to it is broken—and alive to God—living in unbroken fellowship with Him (Romans 6:11).
- I am more than a conqueror (Romans 8:37).
- I overcame the enemy (Revelation 12:11).
- I have everything I need to live a godly life (2 Peter 1:3-4).
- I am an ambassador for Christ (2 Corinthians 5:20). I am part of a chosen generation, a royal priesthood, a holy nation, and a purchased people (1 Peter 2:9).
- I am the righteousness of God—I have right standing with Him in Jesus Christ (2 Corinthians 5:21).
- My body is a temple of the Holy Spirit; I belong to Him (1 Corinthians 6:19).
- I am the light of the world (Matthew 5:14).
- I am redeemed (Deuteronomy 28:15-68; Galatians 3:13).
- I am healed and whole in Jesus (Isaiah 53:5; 1 Peter 2:24).
- I am greatly loved by God (John 3:16; Ephesians 2:4; Colossians 3:12; 1 Thessalonians 1:4).
- I am strengthened with all power according to His glorious might (Colossians 1:11).
- I am not ruled by fear because the Holy Spirit lives in me and gives me His power, love, and self-control (2 Timothy 1:7).

- Christ lives in me, and I live by faith in Him and His love for me (Galatians 2:20).
- I am enough (the Bible).

> **table talk**
>
> How might being good enough help you in your present situation or relationships?
>
> Read and know this:
> *You are seen by God. Let Him see you.*
>   *You are recognized by God. Let Him recognize you.*
>   *You are qualified in God. Let Him qualify you.*
>   *You are good enough with God. Let Him use you.*

you are worthy.

My wife and I were once invited to a fancy dinner by an uppity friend. In a sense, we were invited to their table. The invitation said, "...formal affair, dress appropriately, no kids allowed..." so we knew it would be grandiloquent. We were excited but also a little bit nervous.[70]

Would we fit in?

Is what we are wearing formal enough, or is it too formal?

Are we going to make a fool out of ourselves?

We aren't used to this kind of stuff!

My wife and I spent nearly an hour getting ready, each looking in the mirror fifteen times to make sure we looked appropriate. Embarrassingly, before we walked into the house, we took deep breaths, looked into each other's eyes, and said, "We got this." [71]

It ended up being fine. Worry is a waste of time.

---

[70] Because I am kind of a kid. Would they find me out?!
[71] Third world problems?

Sometimes, being invited to the table brings up fear or anxiety. People often feel they have to have everything together before they go to church, join a bible study, or even sit at God's table.[72]

But let me remind you:
 You are seen,
  you are chosen,
   you are enough,
    and you are worthy.

Psalm 23's opening line is:
 The Lord is my shepherd; I lack nothing.

When the Lord is your shepherd, you are worthy. When you sit at the table, you have all that you need.

***

wor·thy
adjective

1. having or showing the qualities or abilities that merit recognition in a specified way.

According to the dictionary, synonyms for "worthy" are "valuable," "admirable," "precious," and "worthwhile." Would you describe yourself in this way?

As you know, I am a dad. I have these two nearly perfect humans that my wife and I somehow made. I love them

---

[72] What a nasty lie this is. I will never have it all together.

so much. But you know what hurts? It pains me when they struggle with self-confidence or self-doubt. We just celebrated the end of the school year, and the other day, my daughter was sharing with my wife how she felt that no one would miss her over the summer. I hear this, and it breaks my heart.

I wonder how painful it is for God to see us when we feel worthless.

We often get stuck reading this part:

> *For all have sinned and fall short of the glory of God...*[73]

Which is true.

We are all messed up. We are not worthy at all to sit at the table.

We are pretty dirty when left to our own devices.

But then, we get to read the next line:

> *...and all are justified freely by his grace through the redemption that came by Christ Jesus.*[74]

"Justified" is another way to say "to be made worthy."
You have been made worthy.

When my kids are feeling down, I do my best to tell them how much I love them and think highly of them. I do this to help them see themselves the way I see them.

---

[73] Romans 3:23. This passage is often used by a sweating, yelling preacher in a suit.
[74] Romans 3:24.

I feel like our spiritual Father does the same:

> *The Lord your God is with you, the Mighty Warrior who saves. He will take great delight in you; in His love he will no longer rebuke you, but will rejoice over you with singing.*[75]

The Lord rejoices over us.
    It seems "unworthy"
        is the opposite of
            how God sees you.

                He sees you worthy of
                a seat at His table.

***

I like superhero movies.[76] *Avengers* and *Justice League* are some of my favorites because they both take these incredible superheroes and put them on a team. I love that each of these superheroes has something significant to bring to the table, and they all have these crazy, unique superpowers.

    Whenever I watch superhero movies, I come out of the theater looking for someone to save.[77] I come walking out with my chest puffed up. But one day, a harrowing thought came over me. *I would never be chosen for the Avengers.* I am not the Hulk, I am not Thor, I am not Captain America,

---

[75] Zephaniah 3:17.

[76] Personally, I am a Marvel guy, but can dig some Batman and Superman action every now and then.

[77] This isn't just me… is it?

and I am not even rich enough to build a sweet iron suit. I am just David—nothing spectacular, nothing incredible. As a matter of fact, I am very imperfect and messed up. But imagine a man slips me a note. It says, "David, we need you. We need your skills, your talent, and your muscle for the Avengers. Would you consider being part of this team?"

I would be like... "Um, yeah... but how? What do I have to offer?"

Whether you are a company CEO, a parent working hard to raise your kids, a middle school dropout, or someone who generally feels like you screwed up, the message of being worthy is for everyone. And by everyone, I mean *anyone*.

We see a common theme throughout the scriptures: God often chooses the unworthy and insignificant to do the significant.

Moses

When I think of Moses, I think of a strong, confident bearded man holding up his hands to part the Red Sea.[78] Yet, Moses didn't believe he was fit to lead. He had low self-confidence. When God spoke to Moses to go to Pharaoh, he responded:

> *Who am I that I should go to Pharaoh, and that I should bring the children of Israel out of Egypt?*[79]

"Who am I?"

---

[78] That's what he looks like in the pictures. Imagine we get to heaven one day and he has a handlebar mustache.

[79] Exodus 3:11.

In other words, "I am a nobody. Why would *I* go to see the Pharaoh? I am not worthy." Yet, God used him to free an entire people group from slavery.

On top of that, when it came to speaking, Moses was not the most eloquent public speaker around. Some scholars reference this next line to say he had some sort of speech impediment:

> Moses said to the LORD, "Pardon your servant, Lord. I have never been eloquent, neither in the past nor since you have spoken to your servant. I am slow of speech and tongue."[80]

Yet, Moses had some incredible moments speaking to the Israelites. God had chosen someone and was qualifying someone who was flawed, imperfect, and didn't believe they could carry out one of the most significant events in Jewish history—but God did.

Mary

God chose Mary to be the one to bring the King of kings into the world. Mary was just an ordinary girl. Most scholars point out that she was anywhere from twelve to sixteen years old when she was chosen by God. Mary was also a girl—a little girl. In ancient times, women did not have a large role in society. I do not have to go into crazy depth about this, but women (let alone younger girls) were often seen as the man's property. They had no community significance; they

---

[80] Exodus 4:10.

kept the family together while the men worked, voted, and made decisions. She had no degree or importance and wouldn't have been considered worthy of a seat at the table.

Yet the Lord, in all of His wisdom, chose this woman, who some might deem worthless, to do the impossible and to be the vessel of hope to the world.

Let's spend a moment with Mary.

An angel appears to her and shares a message that she will have a baby called the Son of the Most High. The angel then says, "Guess what? You are the mom, the one bringing this man into the world. You're going to be pregnant!"[81]

This would be happy news to most, but to Mary, this was impossible. Not only physically,[82] but likely mentally, as I wonder if she dealt with her own feelings of unworthiness.

I am sure Mary had questions, and I am sure Mary had doubts, but this is how she responded:

I am the Lord's servant.
May everything happen that you said.[83]

She pretty much said, "Okay, if you say so. I am not so sure about me, but I guess I trust you."

There is a humble trust that takes place here. Mary's response is not in her brain, but in her heart.[84] She knows the character and power of God. She has heard of His promises.

---

[81] Surprise! When's the baby shower?
[82] Scripture says that she was a virgin. I'll leave it there.
[83] Luke 1:38.
[84] Sometimes using your heart more than your head gets people in trouble, but this time it worked out.

She doesn't fight or cower. She accepts it, even if it doesn't make sense. This insignificant, common, worthless woman was chosen to carry out the most significant event in history.

God so often chooses the unlikeliest candidates to fulfill His work and mission. He sees past the man or woman standing before Him and He sees potential.

He sees eternity.

He utilizes the available and the willing.

It doesn't matter if you can't talk or if you're a girl. It doesn't matter if you feel useless or unworthy. You have a spot at His table.

Here's a short roll call of biblical figures and their shortcomings:

Adam and Eve were gullible. Noah was old.

Jonah was stubborn. Gideon was unsure. Jacob was deceptive.

Abraham tried his own plans. David was a murderer.

Solomon was a womanizer.

Elijah was weird.

John the Baptist ate bugs.[85]

It's even more evident when God came to earth as Jesus Christ. As Jesus chose His team, He had similar standards.

---

[85] One time, a fly flew into my coffee and I drank it.

Team Jesus

Jesus didn't pick out the cleanest or the most suited for a spot on His team. He wasn't looking at worthiness; He looked at the willing.

Typically, Jesus chose the ones that others may have scoffed at. In ancient times, rabbis were the primary teachers of scripture, but they were also much more than that. They gave opportunity and life to the young Jews; many called the rabbis "life-givers."[86] Aspiring students didn't get to select a rabbi; it was the other way around. When a rabbi selected a young student, their future was secured. It's almost like being accepted into an Ivy League University, but better. It was a moment of celebration for the family that a rabbi would find a son worthy of teaching. It was rare, unique, and admirable. It meant you were accepted and worthy of instruction. These chosen people became disciples of this rabbi: doing life with their rabbi, eating and living with them.

A rabbi was meant to have disciples. Disciples were followers, imitators, and students of these rabbis. Rabbis were only interested in good stock. Students were needed to grow their school of understanding, their following, and their future, so whatever students they selected would be their future reputation.[87] Rabbis would only choose the best of the best.

But Jesus, who many consider a teacher, was a rabbi who took a different approach. This rabbi walked around and

---

[86] If only teachers in America had this kind of respect.
[87] And retirement!

found willing people and asked them to follow Him. As Rabbi Jesus chose His disciples, He didn't go for the cream-of-the-crop types.

He didn't choose the influencers of the day.

He didn't choose the rich.

He didn't choose the worthy.

He went for a fisherman. He went for a tax collector. He went for a thief. He went for misfits. He went for the ones others would look past.

The Fish Guys

In today's context, professional fishermen are usually seen as pretty cool guys.[88] But being a fisherman in ancient Israel was no special or desired job. As stated earlier, it was the worker's class—the uneducated.

For some reason, Jesus had a soft spot for fishermen.

> *Jesus was walking by the Sea of Galilee. He saw two brothers. They were Simon (his other name was Peter) and Andrew, his brother. They were putting a net into the sea for they were fishermen. Jesus said to them, "Follow Me. I will make you fish for men!" At once they left their nets and followed Him.*
>
> *Going from there, Jesus saw two other brothers. They were James and John, the sons of Zebedee. They were sitting in a boat with their father,*

---

[88] Have you seen the show *River Monsters*? Cool dudes.

> *mending their nets. Jesus called them. At once they left the boat and their father and followed Jesus.*[89]

Jesus chose these men based on their willing hearts, not their resumes. I can imagine the other prestigious rabbis or priests watching as Jesus was recruiting at the lake, probably laughing to themselves. Most rabbis of the day were followed by their clean-cut disciples, and here was a rabbi recruiting at the dump.

Peter, Andrew, James, and John had a spot at the table. Jesus didn't care what they did or how they smelled.

The Tax Guys

Another of Jesus' first followers was a tax collector named Levi. Tax collectors in ancient times were some of the most hated, corrupt individuals. These were the sellouts working for the foreign government, often taking their share from friends and family. Tax collectors were bottom-of-the-barrel types. The term "tax collector" was even used as an insult: "Don't be such a tax collector."[90] Typically, they were cheaters.

>> Traitors.

>> Backstabbers.

In comes Levi, onto the stage of God.

> *Once again, Jesus went out beside the lake. A large crowd came to him, and he began to*

---

[89] Matthew 4:18-22.

[90] I dare you to use that next time you get in an argument. You will hear all the "oohs."

teach them. As he walked along, he saw Levi, son of Alphaeus, sitting at the tax collector's booth. "Follow me," Jesus told him, and Levi got up and followed him. While Jesus was having dinner at Levi's house, many tax collectors and sinners were eating with him and his disciples, for there were many who followed him. When the teachers of the law, who were Pharisees, saw him eating with the sinners and tax collectors, they asked his disciples: "Why does he eat with tax collectors and sinners?" On hearing this, Jesus said to them, "It is not the healthy who need a doctor, but the sick. I have not come to call the righteous, but sinners."[91]

Two quick notes: One, these "tax collectors" are explicitly comparative to sinners, and two, Jesus simply didn't care what others thought.[92] He walks straight up to this unworthy tax collector and says, "Follow me." What prompted Jesus to do this? It doesn't appear that Jesus and Levi knew each other beforehand, but it did seem that Jesus knew the potential of a willing heart.

Sometimes that's all it takes.

I can imagine the religious leaders watching this new rabbi choosing scum of the earth to be His followers in disgust. In their minds, these guys were not worth it. But I believe God believes in second, third, fourth, and fifth chances.

---

[91] Mark 2:13-17.
[92] Mark 2:16.

There was one time some church leaders straight-up asked about why Jesus was recruiting these types of people:

> "Why does he eat with tax collectors and sinners?"[93]

In response, He replied,

> ...the healthy don't need a doctor; the sick do.[94]

He recognizes the illness, but He also sees past it.
As a matter of fact, He targets it.

One day, He tells these church leaders a story about a tax collector. He starts with two men who walked into the temple to pray:

> ...one a Pharisee and the other a tax collector. The Pharisee stood by himself and prayed: "God, I thank you that I am not like other people—robbers, evildoers, adulterers—or even like this tax collector. I fast twice a week and give a tenth of all I get." But the tax collector stood at a distance. He would not even look up to heaven, but beat his breast and said, "God, have mercy on me, a sinner."

Jesus looks upon his listeners and says,

---

[93] It's a great way of life.
[94] Mark 2:17.

> *I tell you that this man, rather than the other, went home justified before God.*[95]

Jesus finishes his story by saying that the tax collector was the one that went home justified and worthy that day. This statement would have made any listener's jaw hit the ground. They would never say anything close to that about these types of people: the unworthy.

Not long after, a man named Zacchaeus (another tax collector hated by the people) comes into the picture. Jesus was walking through the streets when the scene took place. Zacchaeus was a short guy who was trying to see Jesus. He had heard of the rabbi who had a following of his own kind. He climbed a tree to try to sneak a peek at this mysterious rabbi who loves tax guys, and Jesus walked straight up to him and said, "Zacchaeus, come down from there!"

Jesus ended up having dinner with the man while all of the onlookers looked at him with disgust.

Levi and Zacchaeus had a spot at the table. Jesus didn't mind the reputation they carried.

They were worthy in the eyes of Jesus.

The Thief

Judas Iscariot was a son of some wealthy Jewish parents. He had started exploring the teachings of John the Baptist and his parents had disowned him. He was looking for employment when Jesus' disciples found him.

---

[95] Luke 18:9-14.

Judas, the twelfth disciple, was invited to the table by Jesus.

He was the best-educated man among the twelve and a good thinker, but not always an honest thinker. Now, if you know anything about Judas, you probably know him as the one who ends up being the bad guy.[96] We know that, but the disciples did not. What's fascinating is that Jesus knew the fate of Judas.

Jesus knew Judas' heart.
Jesus knew what would take place in the years to come.

Talk about unworthy.

He would not only royally mess up a few years later, but Judas reportedly stole often from the finances of the disciples and Jesus. One day, Judas was trying to lecture another follower of Jesus by asking,

> Why wasn't this perfume sold for three hundred denarii and the money given to the poor?[97]

The text then describes:

> Judas did not say this because he cared about the poor, but because he was a thief. As keeper of the money bag, he used to take from what was put into it.[98]

---

[96] Even the name Judas makes some people squirm.
[97] John 12:5.
[98] John 12:6.

Meaning he helped himself to the money.

Secretly.

He was a thief.

Yet, he was part of team Jesus. He had a spot. Jesus, in His knowledge, knew of his unworthiness. Still, there was a chair for Judas at the table.

God does things a little backward. He chooses the players that no one else wants on the team. He chose the students that no other teacher thought worthy.

This theme hasn't changed throughout the history of unworthiness.

A few years later, there's this guy...

The Misfit

There was a man named Saul—not Saul from the Old Testament, but Saul from the New Testament. He later goes by the name Paul; you may have heard of him. He was a pretty hard dude.[99] He was, as he called himself, a "Hebrew of Hebrews," which would be consistent with someone in our modern day saying that they are part of the Aryan race.[100] This would have been a very proud statement about his nationality. His family was a devout Jewish household, and he grew up believing his poopoo didn't stink.

---

[99] Meaning tough and scary, not physically hard. But who knows?
[100] Perverted ideology in which Nordic or White races (predominantly among German and other northern European peoples) are deemed the highest in racial hierarchy. Saul was sort of like Hitler.

Saul was trained in respected Jewish schools under the most prestigious rabbis, but something about these Jewish schools was in stark contrast to this rabbi, Jesus. These men did not like Jesus or His following. These early Jewish leaders regarded Jesus as false and believed He was hurting their mission. Saul believed Jesus to be a crazy heretic. Therefore, to rid the rot of the pure Jewish faith, Saul saw any believer in Jesus as an attack of the purity of his nationality.

The book of Acts says that Saul "breathed out" murderous threats to the followers of Jesus. Not sure what breathing out murderous threats means, but it can't be good.[101]

He hated Jesus.
Definitely not worthy of a seat at His table.

Let's fast-forward to a little later, after Jesus died. Saul is still around, hating on Jesus and His followers. He was on his way to a city called Damascus to arrest any followers he could find, but it was on this road that Jesus chose Saul.

He would give worth to he who was unworthy.

To summarize the scene, Jesus appears like a bright light and blinds Saul. Around that same time, the Lord speaks to a Jewish believer named Ananias in Damascus about Saul. God tells Ananias to go and meet Saul to commission him: to invite him to the table.

Now remember, Ananias is one of the believers that Saul was on his way to put in prison for his beliefs. I can understand his reservations.

---

[101] Acts 9. Sounds to me like bad onion breath.

> "Lord," Ananias answered, "I have heard many reports about this man and all the harm he has done to your holy people in Jerusalem. And he has come here with authority from the chief priests to arrest all who call on your name."
>
> But the Lord said to Ananias, "Go! This man is my chosen instrument to proclaim my name to the Gentiles and their kings and to the people of Israel."[102]

Ananias had a legitimate response. He was thinking, *Lord, you're crazy! This dude's mission is to destroy me, my family, and my friends. Why would I go pray for him? He shouldn't have a seat at the table.*

God's response: "Because he is worth it."

This is the character of our God. Little did Ananias know that Saul would later go by the name Paul and revolutionize the world for Jesus Christ.

It doesn't matter who you are,
> what you have done,
>> or what you haven't done.
>>> God wants you to be part of His team.
>>> He wants you at His table.

>>>> In your unworthiness, the presence of Jesus makes you worthy.

---

[102] Acts 9:13-15.

> He finds you worthy, but are you willing?

The fishermen left their nets, boats, and possibly their life's work behind. Levi left his tax booth, probably loaded with money, and walked after this rabbi who called him out. Zacchaeus left his tree and made some incredible commitments. Judas, with his dark future, was called to the team and decided to follow the rabbi. Paul bypassed his Hebrew reputation and devoted his life to Jesus. Did they see something special in this new rabbi, or did they, deep down, feel seen, feel wanted, and feel included? We will never know, but what we do know is that these men were honored when nobody else seemed to honor them. They were recognized when their recognition was sour. They were chosen when others looked at them in anger and disgust, and they were given life when others wished the worst upon them.

They were celebrated as worthy, even in their unworthiness.

Then There's This Guy: Me

Way back when I was in college, there was a season when I had a lot going for me. I was student body president, captain of the university baseball team, and dating the school beauty.[103]

This was also around the time I began truly following Jesus. I led a weekly chapel for the school and decided to get my degree in Bible. I became the school's student-pastor.

---

[103] That school beauty became my future wife.

> I was the poster boy, golden child of the school.

The university hosted an annual Thanksgiving luncheon that was kind of a big deal. Each department chair had the opportunity to invite one student to sit at the table, and you guessed it, I was invited. Most would look at the resume I was sporting and say, "Yep, it makes sense for a guy like that to be a worthy candidate for a spot at a distinguished table."

But...

It was the week before the luncheon. I had a large research paper due in my "Religions of the World" class. Back in those days, I was a bit of a procrastinator,[104] but this time, I kind of forgot.

So, the day it was due, I started doing what I had learned to do so well: cramming some weak work together to finish. I remember scrambling to get a certain page length, copying and pasting to fill the space. I finally finished.

Not my best work and not *really* my own words,

>> but the paper was done.

No need to proofread; I'll be fine. The professor will never know.

I turned it in.

I turned in a highly "borrowed" paper without so much as the blink of an eye.

---

[104] Rita Mae Brown defines procrastination as "proactively delaying the implementation of the energy-intensive phase of the project until the enthusiasm factor is at its maximum effectiveness."

the table.

Within a few hours, I get an email from my professor, the department chair, that reads,
"David, would you come to my office?"

That was it. That was all the email said. This was also the guy who invited me to that prestigious Thanksgiving table. Here's how clueless I was: I had no idea what the email was about—I just knew it was serious. Maybe it was about what we were going to wear to the luncheon?

When I got to his office, he had my research paper with highlighted sections in one hand; in the other hand, he had a printed article with other highlighted areas.

Instantly, fear wraps around my mind. Some of the paragraphs were exactly the same. In my rush, I plagiarized. I stole words and claimed them to be my own. This is not good. Plagiarism can result in a failed grade or course and, depending on the school, expulsion. It's an offense that instantly deems a student unworthy of a degree or even an opportunity at the institution.

Remember: this is the year I had the titles, the glory, and a lot going for me. Instantly, my fate was in the hands of this man. I went from hero to zero in a moment.

The professor looked at me.

He looked at me and said, "You've plagiarized. The consequences can be severe. This work is unworthy, but I know it's not who you are. I know you, and I know your heart. I will give you another chance. Go home and write me a paper and turn it in tomorrow." I was blown away.

As I left the room, he said, "David, remember who you are; all is good and erased." The shredder sounded in the background. "And by the way, I'm still hoping to see you seated next to me at the table for Thanksgiving."

I went home, dazzled and confused, but so, so grateful. I went straight to work and stayed up late, but I wrote one of the best research papers I had ever written.

Some call it lucky, some call it a privilege, but I call it mercy. Mercy shown to an unworthy recipient.

I learned a big lesson that day.

Despite any feelings you may have of shame and unworthiness, someone who truly knows and cares for you can see beyond that. They choose to see you as deserving.

Worthy.

> In my mess-up, I was still seen and invited to the table.

The year went on, and this professor of mine became one of my closest mentors. It's funny; after that day, he never once brought up the plagiarism, and I never did it again.

***

Let me finish the chapter with a recount of a story Jesus told. It was about a young man who made serious mistakes with his father and his household. You may have heard of him; he's been made biblically famous. He is nicknamed the prodigal son. If you are unfamiliar with the story, please pause this reading and read Luke 15:11-32.

the table.

I love the scene when he comes home.

> ...while he was still a long way off, his father saw him and was filled with compassion for him; he ran to his son, threw his arms around him, and kissed him.
> The son said to him, "Father, I have sinned against heaven and against you. I am no longer worthy to be called your son."
> But the father said to his servants, "Quick! Bring the best robe and put it on him. Put a ring on his finger and sandals on his feet. Bring the fattened calf and kill it. Let's have a feast and celebrate."[105]

Did you catch it?
He was no longer worthy, yet he still had a place at the table. The father *sees* him and has compassion for him. He throws his arms around him and kisses him. The father prepares a table.

The young man sits at the table
    with the best robe,
        with new jewelry and shoes,
            with the finest food,

                to feast.

The number one heart's desire of our Father is to make us worthy and have us at His

---

[105] Luke 15:20-22.

Then There's You

God chose you in your imperfections. He sees past your resume, mistakes, mess-ups, illnesses, and unworthiness. Jesus sees you and intimately knows you. He sees everything about you, even the darkest and unworthiest parts about you—but he gives you worth anyway.

I titled this chapter "You Are Worthy,"
        but it should be, "You Are *Made* Worthy."

                Because that's really it.

table talk

Take two minutes to listen and truly hear God.

Have a conversation with yourself and with God.

How do you see yourself?

Pause for a moment and think about it. What thoughts have you had about your self-worth today?

Then,

imagine God's hand reaching out to you,
        wiping you clean.
           Let Him make you worthy
        today.

you are adopted.

A bottle of water is pretty interesting.

I can buy one at a grocery store for about twenty-five cents. I can walk into a gas station and purchase a bottle for a dollar. If I went to a concert, I'd pay about three dollars. When I am on an airplane, they will charge me six. Yet, in some places, it is absolutely free.
The only thing that changes the water bottle's value is its location.

That's life.

The thing about the table is that our seat carries our value. Our place at the table is priceless, and we really don't deserve one. After all, it is a king's table. A king's table is mainly reserved for his nobles or advisors, but it is also reserved for his kids.

And scripture says that we have been accepted, anointed, and adopted.

You anoint my head with oil.[106]

In ancient Israel, anointing someone with oil meant a few different things: it was often for the physically sick or spiritually ill, but there was also the traditional use of oil as an honor. Anointing someone with oil was customary among the ancient Hebrews as a practice of welcoming someone to their home for a meal or even to stay. Anointing someone with oil would have been seen as an act of hospitality and shown respect to esteemed visitors. As David the Psalmist wrote these lines, he regarded himself as the Lord's special guest sitting at His table.

But here is the twist: We are not just guests at the Lord's table. Anointing someone with oil was also used to symbolize them being a long-term resident of a home. In other words, it was like taking someone in as their own.

It goes on to say:
...and I will dwell in the house of the Lord forever.[107]

Forever is a big word. David understood that he was not merely a short-term visitor who would share a meal once and leave for good. Nor would he be invited to return for dinner only occasionally. David experienced a life of a continual place setting at the table. He recognized that having a seat was tantamount to being anointed and adopted into a family. The anointing

---

[106] Psalm 23:5.
[107] Psalm 23:6.

at the table represented sonship. He was not a guest, but a permanent family member.[108]

God becomes our everlasting Father.

Having a seat at the table represents
    being accepted,
        being anointed,
           being adopted.

***

I have a friend.
He has the most loving family.

For the longest time, I would look at his family and think to myself, *How perfect are they?* One day, while playing backyard basketball together, I could tell he was off. As I probed, he told me he was going to meet his dad for the first time later that evening and was nervous about it. This caught me off-guard. I had no idea what he was talking about. I laughed, but he looked serious.
He looked at me and said, "*Biological* father."
I stopped laughing.

    He was adopted. I never would've known.

He began to tell me that the man I believed was his dad was not his birth father. I was stunned. As I recall, when Dad number one left, Dad number two came into the picture. Dad number two went through a legal process to adopt this

---

[108] Can you imagine if a family was finite? You go to your parent's dinner table this evening and they say, "Actually, no, not today. You're not my kid today. Maybe tomorrow."

young child, and Dad number one ran for the hills, never to partake in his son's upbringing. Tragic as it was, this event left room for Dad number two and a privileged upbringing.[109]

There is something very special about adoption. Adoption is taking someone who does not have a mom or a dad and saying, "I choose you. You are now my son or my daughter. I am your mom; I am your dad." You are taking the parentless and giving them parents.

This is what the table represents.

I have some friends who went through the process of adoption. We had an up close and personal seat to witness the adoption operation. By no means is it easy.[110]

Not able to have biological children, they were looking to adopt. It took years, but it finally happened. They were so full of tears and joy. They adopted him when he was just a few months old, and what they were able to provide for this child was amazing. They offered a life to this child that he would never have gotten if left to his own.

Then it happened.[111] They got pregnant. They ended up birthing a child years later while their adopted son was starting elementary school. The way this little boy took the newborn into his arms as his brother was breathtaking—a true definition of family and love. The parents ended up having more biological children, and it was so beautiful to

---

[109] That got confusing real quick. I could have used the word "man." The name "dad" should be earned.

[110] Or cheap.

[111] Of course. Right?

see that there was no difference between them all in love or value. They all had seats at their dinner table.

Children are pretty awesome.[112]

There is this fascinating scene where the disciples of Jesus argued with each other about who was the best.[113] They then turn to ask Jesus, who they thought would settle their argument, about it.

"*Who is the greatest?*"[114] they asked.[115]

But then, Jesus does something unexpected. He calls a child over to stand among them. Who was this child? No clue. Most likely some random kid walking by.[116] Then, Jesus said,

> *I tell you the truth, unless you change and become like little children, you will never enter the kingdom of heaven.*[117]

As we know, in the social hierarchy of ancient Israel, men were on top. Women didn't have too much value, but the children had even less. Children were low on the totem pole because they didn't do anything productive. They were

---

[112] Being in education for over a decade, I would hope I say that.

[113] Like when all the students ask the teacher who their favorite is. I like to keep my students in suspense.

[114] Matthew 18:1.

[115] I wonder if Judas was part of this argument?

[116] In my imagination, this kid has red hair, freckles, no shoes, and dirty feet. I don't know why. That's just the type of kid my brain pictures Jesus calling to His disciples.

[117] Matthew 18:3.

weak, dependent, useless kids, fully reliant on parents for everything.[118] But to Jesus, this child was the greatest.

This moment would have been strange to the people around Jesus.
    Acceptance and anointing had to do with one's value.
               Kids were not "great."

Yet, here is a rabbi who does things differently.
    Jesus invited his disciples to be dependent on Him.
        Jesus invited his followers to be adopted.

In your weakness, He is strong.[119]

It doesn't matter what you do, how much you study, or what your title is. God has chosen and chooses to adopt *everyone*—even you. And He thinks it's pretty great to rely on Him.

***

In any society, adoption is beautiful. Adopting children holds so much value, and typically, it's young kids who are chosen. But have you ever seen someone who was legally adopted as an adult? Absolutely heart-wrenching. This event is not done for parental supervision. This circumstance is not for provision. This is not to throw a ball around in the backyard.[120] Adult adoption represents something deeper;

---

[118] As I reread that, it sounds pretty harsh.
[119] 2 Corinthians 12:9-10.
[120] Although, that would be fun.

it represents family. It represents acceptance. It represents devotion.

> It represents a seat at the table.

I heard a fantastic story about a seventy-six-year-old woman who was adopted. This would make most people do a double take, but isn't it pretty cool? Can you imagine the spread at their dinner party that night?[121]

> This happens all the time in the kingdom of heaven.

According to the scriptures,

> ...He knows everything.[122]

If that is true, and we truly believe God knows all and knows you and what you would become before you were even born, then you've been accepted, even with everything you've already done and will do. You were picked to be adopted with your whole life on record.[123]

It's like that old flea-infested, dirty, wretched dog that sits in the cage at the back of the pound. Every family that walks through to pick a pet chooses the younger, cuter ones. This dog is overlooked.[124] That dog usually lays in the corner, thinking no one will ever choose him. But one day, a wealthy

---

[121] According to the Guinness Book of World Records, the oldest adopted person is Mary Banks-Smith (aged 76 years 96 days) when she was officially adopted by Muriel Banks Clayton in Dallas, Texas, USA, on June 9th, 2015.

[122] 1 John 3:20.

[123] Have you ever imagined your life was a movie that other people get to watch? Interesting concept. If you have yet to see Jim Carrey's *The Truman Show*, that's the premise. Pretty wild.

[124] I can hear Sarah McLachlan begin to sing.

family walks in, walks straight to the cage, and says, "We want this one." The keeper even tries to talk them out of it and show them younger, cleaner dogs, but they say, "No, we want this dog."

You are that dog.

> God knows your entire life.

Every piece of it. The parts you are proud of and the parts that make you uneasy. He even sees that day that you trashed Him, and He says, "This is the one. This is the one I want to adopt into my family. This is the one I want to bear my name."

We already know:
> For he chose us in him before the creation of the world to be holy and blameless in his sight....[125]

But this next line is the gut-puncher:
> ...In love, he predestined us for adoption to sonship through Jesus Christ, in accordance with his pleasure and will.[126]

According to His pleasure and according to His will, you were adopted.

> God delights in you,
> and it has nothing to do
> with what you do, but has

---
[125] Ephesians 1:4.
[126] Ephesians 1:5.

everything to do with your adoption.

Adoption is powerful. In any culture, to adopt is to give new life. But in the context in which these lines were written in ancient Rome, adoption was a very significant decision. Check out some facts about Roman adoption:

- First, the adopted person lost all their rights with their old family. On the other hand, they gained those same rights back with their new family. They received a new name and a new family.
- Second, the adoptee became heir to the father's estate.
- Third, the old life of the adopted person was completely wiped out; they were regarded as a new person entering a new life that the past had nothing to do with.

Who I was before I came into my new family had no effect on my new identity. I inherited a family. I inherited a rich history of grandparents and great-grandparents. I am a part of something I never dreamed of that is bigger than myself. My old life has nothing on me.

- Finally, in the eyes of the law, the adopted child was seen as an absolute child of the new father whether the adoptee had a family or not. Once the adoption takes place, you have a family. You have a name.

God is a father to the fatherless.[127]

---
[127] Psalm 68:5.

In case you are unfamiliar with adoption, who picks who? It's not the kid who picks the parents. The parents pick the kids. You have been picked out of the crowd. You have been chosen to be adopted, just like that little kid walking down the street when Jesus called him over and said, "This, my friends, this represents the greatest."

In Roman adoption, the adoptee gets a new identity. His old obligations and debts are wiped out, and new obligations are assumed. Each and every one of us is chosen and adopted as the sons and daughters of the King.

The King looked at you and said, "You are the one."

> We have been adopted into the family.

> > We have a seat at the table.

***

I love the storyline of the play and movie *Annie*.[128] A poor orphan girl is chosen and legally adopted by one of the richest men in the city. Automatically, everything that was his is now hers. One second she is poor and has nothing; the next moment, she has it all.

> It is the same with you.

> *You are no longer a slave but God's own child. And since you are his child, God has made you his heir.*[129]

---

[128] It's a hard-knock life for us.
[129] Galatians 4:7.

We go from a slave to an heir.[130] You get to inherit what is God's; you become an heir to the King. That makes you a prince. A princess.

> Royalty.

In the movie *Mr. Deeds*, the character played by Adam Sandler portrays someone who inherits an incredible amount of money by surprise. One day, he was a poor worker in a small town, and the next, he was one of the richest men in the country. That's an image of what we are invited to, what we were chosen for—a godly inheritance.

But the table is not about what you'll get—it's about what you already have. You inherited a good dad, a family, and the power of the Holy Spirit. Those are happenings that are for right now. You already received what the Father has: love, joy, peace, patience, kindness, goodness, faithfulness, gentleness, and self-control. It's yours right now! You are a child in God's family. You are given the riches of his grace: kindness, patience, glory, wisdom, power, and mercy.[131]

We also inherit an abundant life as well as a future life free from worry and harm. A seat at this incredible dinner table is ours and forever ours. What an inheritance! You are far richer than you realize, which is why Paul could write with confidence:

---

[130] Not a *hair*, an *heir*. They have similar spelling and pronunciation but completely different meanings. Thank God.
[131] Ephesians 1:7; Romans 2:4; 9:23; 11:33; Ephesians 3:16; 2:4.

> *My God will meet all your needs according to his glorious riches in Christ Jesus.*[132]

You are seen, chosen, made worthy, and then adopted by the King. You are royalty! So here's a question for you: When you go through your front door, are you walking into the orphanage, or are you walking into the palace? Are you eating royal food from the King's court or settling for scraps? Are you walking around in ragtag clothes or wearing clothes fit for a prince or a princess?

> Are you seated at the table
> or sitting on the dirt?

We did nothing to earn it; we did nothing to deserve it. God, the great Father and adopter, in His amazing love and mercy for you, has taken you just as you are and adopted you. Your mess-ups are cleaned, and that unearned love and glory are inherited.

***

So, what's the catch? What is the price of adoption? Doesn't it always seem like there is a catch with the good things in life?

> There is, technically, a catch for your adoption.

> Most would say it is too good to be true. But the price for

---

[132] Philippians 4:19.

> this incredible adoption is a decision. It's belief.

> *For you are all sons and daughters of God through faith in Christ Jesus.*[133]

We become sons and daughters adopted into the family of Christ and invited to the table based on a decision. Based on faith. That's it.

And yes, there is a cost. And it is a lot.

Scripture says that we have all messed up and deserve death. We have all fallen short of perfection, and boy, is that true.[134] In ancient times, across different religions, they often offered a sacrifice to the gods or even the God of scriptures to pay for their sins. The Old Testament is full of regulations on what one would owe to cleanse themselves of sin. As a matter of fact, there were two types of sacrifices found in ancient times: the voluntary sacrifice and the mandatory sacrifice. Voluntary sacrifices include offerings expressing your praise for God. This would be done out of one's goodwill. Meanwhile, the mandatory sacrifices outlined in scripture were required for cleanliness. They were doves, cows, or, in some extreme cultural cases, children. The severity of your mess-up and your social situation would dictate how you would make it right with the divine.[135] From minor and small

---

[133] Galatians 3:26.

[134] Can I insert the little emoji of the guy with his hand up?

[135] So that time you had that little white lie about eating all of your food, you might've had to sacrifice a bug. But that time you blamed your sister for breaking the window? Sorry, Fluffy. Oh, and don't get me started on that time you cussed.

sacrifices to large and significant ones, how you would pay for sin was a huge deal to these ancient people.

Yet, this ancient book, the Bible, claims there was an ultimate sacrifice to make us right with God. It was the perfect and final sacrifice of a pure man: the Son of God, Jesus Christ. He came to pay for our sins, to make us pure as the clear waters of the High Sierras and white as freshly fallen snow, to wipe away every mess-up we have ever committed as well as the mess-ups to come. He did this through His death on the cross.

> For our adoption, there had to be a sacrifice.

> When they came to arrest Jesus, He didn't fight or flee.[136]

> He was not the victim; He volunteered.

It was His sacrifice.
> He was killed for me.
>> His life was taken for you.

>>> For you and I to be made right with God, a sacrifice to trump all sacrifices had to take place.

Our adoption required the greatest sacrifice,
> but that's not how the story ends.

---

[136] Matthew 26:50. This moment is pretty significant when thinking about the human response of fight or flight.

According to the scriptures, Jesus defeated death. Three days later, He came back to life in victory, proving Himself to be who He said He was—proving Himself to be all-powerful.

God loved you so much that He adopted you, but in order to do that, He had to give His one and only Son, Jesus, to be murdered as a sacrifice. And if you simply believe in Him, believe that Jesus was the Son of God who was sacrificed as a ransom for the sins of humanity, scripture says you will experience an abundant life as an adopted son or daughter.

That's it.

It just takes a little bit of faith on your part.

Many people don't believe it, and they have their reasons. I've been there. I went through a season in my life of questions and an abandonment of faith. I went through anxiety and depression and questioned if God even existed.

Maybe that's you.

And that's okay.

It's normal.

Early in college, I asked a foreign exchange student friend of mine who was Muslim from Saudi Arabia, straight-up, why he followed Islam. He responded, "Because my parents are Muslim, my teachers were Muslim, my friends and family are Muslim, and everyone I know back home is Muslim. Therefore, I am Muslim." He then shot back and asked why I followed Jesus, and I had nothing better to say.[137]

---

[137] I remember feeling fake.

What about you? Why are you reading this book?
If you consider yourself a Christian, then why?

I am sure you, like me, have had some connection to church or Jesus at some point in your life. If you are reading this while living in America, you are residing in a nation that is predominantly considered "Christian" by the world.

But being America's version of Christian doesn't necessarily mean you have met Jesus and decided to follow His life. Going to church doesn't mean you are adopted and sitting at the table. Being a Christian doesn't mean you have met your Dad—your heavenly Father—God.

There is a big difference between the adopted son and daughter sitting at the table and the one who's adopted but still sitting on their bed at the orphanage.

This was me. I was adopted but still walking the streets. I was not sitting at the table.[138]

The conversation with my Muslim friend provoked a hunger for truth in me. This prompted me to pray for the first time in my life. I spoke with God as if He was sitting in my dorm room, asking Him questions like, "Do you even exist?

---

[138] I believe that churches all over the world are full of people who are walking the streets. They haven't actually sat at the table.

the table.

Are you even real?" I began reading the Bible intently for the first time in my life. I read the book of Luke as a critic.[139] I remember getting to the end and having an understanding that Jesus was either crazy or He was really God. I wasn't entirely sure; even to this day, I still have questions, but one of those nights in my dorm room, I decided to take a blind step forward.

> I remember the night.

I prayed, "God, I don't know if this is true, but I choose to believe. Would You help me with my unbelief? I need You, God. I invite You into my life. Would You show yourself?" And He did. I experienced the love and the power of Jesus in such a real way. It began a hunger for truth, God, and a supernatural relationship with my heavenly Father. I began to sense His presence and His guidance with each step I took. I became emboldened by the Holy Spirit, saying things and doing things I didn't know to say or do. My life radically began changing morally, mentally, and emotionally. I began to experience what I would call an abundant life.

> I met Jesus, my Father.
>> I took a seat at the table.
>>> I began to experience Jesus' love and power.
>>>> I was adopted, and I felt it.

The weeks and the months to follow were full of incredible signs and wonders, affirming my belief. All it took was me

---

[139] Try it. Read the book of Luke as if you had never heard the name Jesus in your life.

humbling myself like a child. Asking the tough questions and allowing God to adopt me. It took faith. It took a decision. It took me.

And let me tell you, it's not a one-and-done moment. Every day I wake up and say, "Lord, I am yours. I give my life and today to you."

Every morning that you wake up, you must sit at the right table. Once you sit at the table as an adopted child, it doesn't mean that life is now going to be easy and perfect. Being adopted is challenging sometimes, because life is hard.

But where are you today?

Can I have you try something?

Ask God to show Himself.

I am convinced He is willing and waiting for you.

If my daughter walked into the house and said, "Daddy, if you do a backflip and stand on your head, then I will believe you are real and I will love you." I would feel a little bit weird—maybe even offended. Scripture does say to not put the Lord your God to the test.

But...

If my daughter walked into the house and said, "Daddy, would you come to me? I want to see you." I would rush over to her and embrace her with a hug.

the table.

> There is nothing better than hearing my children wanting to see me and be with me.
>
> It is the same with our heavenly Father.

The book of James says,
> *If you draw close to God, He will draw close to you.*[140]

Asking God to show Himself is not a test; it is simply a plea to your Father to be close to Him. Parents love to be seen and wanted by their kids, and so does our God.
> *...Our Father who art in Heaven.*[141]

Back to my story.
I consider these moments of my life as the days when I was reborn as a follower of Jesus, convinced of His good news of adoption.[142]

Many people in the church circle call this being "born again." Jesus speaks to this notion of being reborn in an interesting conversation with an ancient Jewish official named Nicodemus:

> *Jesus said, "Very truly I tell you, no one can see the kingdom of God unless they are born again."*

---

[140] James 4:8.
[141] Matthew 6:9. Passage taken from the New King James Version.
[142] Notice I said "days." For me, it wasn't just a "moment."

He's pretty much saying you can't sit at the table until you are reborn as an adopted kid.

> *"How can someone be born when they are old?" Nicodemus asked. "Surely they cannot enter a second time into their mother's womb to be born!"*

Good point, my friend. If that were the case, I am sure a whole lot of people wouldn't choose adoption.

> *Jesus answered, "Very truly I tell you, no one can enter the kingdom of God unless they are born of water and the Spirit. Flesh gives birth to flesh, but the Spirit gives birth to spirit. You should not be surprised at my saying, 'You must be born again.' The wind blows wherever it pleases. You hear its sound, but you cannot tell where it comes from or where it is going. So it is with everyone born of the Spirit."*
>
> *"How can this be?" Nicodemus asked.*[143]

I love how Nicodemus questions this.

It is very easy to question. What an odd thing for Jesus to say, "You must be born again." Questionable. But the idea is that once you believe, once you give faith a try, once you are adopted and sit at the table, you are a new person. You have been reborn into a new creation. Your old life is over, and you have initiated something new.

---

[143] John 3:3-9.

> *This means that anyone who belongs to Christ has become a new person. The old life is gone; a new life has begun!*[144]

I will tell you the truth, the man I am today is completely different from the boy I was before having this born-again experience. Many would have described me as timid, shy, a follower, and insecure, but now I hear words like leader, bold, and strong being used to describe me instead. The old is gone, and a new life has begun. It took the pursuit of truth. It took a simple mindset switch of belief.

> Being adopted means being reborn.
>> Being adopted means actually sitting at the table.

Some of you are like Nicodemus, questioning, even as you read these words, "How can this be?"

Good.

It is good to question and to be unsure of things.

Not questioning is like mindlessly following advice from an advertisement. It's not authentic.

I am not sure of anything in this life. In fact, I am full of suspicion and questions. Isn't this the human condition? If you're too sure about something, be wary. Part of being human is having faith and belief. I choose to believe. I decided to take a leap of faith, and I am convinced that because of this simple belief, I am an adopted son of the

---

[144] 2 Corinthians 5:17.

Most High. This is not because of what I have done, but because of what God did through Jesus. Because of Jesus, I have a seat at the table. Because of Jesus, I have been adopted.

> The adoption papers are waiting to be signed.
>> God has already gone through the agonizing adoption process.
>>> It's now up to you. You have to pick up the pen and sign the adoption papers. You have to leave the orphanage, the streets, and the dirt. You have to take your new seat.
>>>> Your new seat at the table.

Quit waiting and be who you are called to be.
God offers a life to you—a life you would never have gotten if left on your own.
> An adopted life.
> An abundant life.

Not everyone is willing to be adopted; not everybody is ready to believe it's that simple. I get it.

But what if?

> What if this ancient book is telling the truth? What if we truly are recognized, chosen, adopted, and invited to join the family? What if there really is a table? What if we truly were invited to sit? What if it was based on a simple decision? A decision to believe.

God prepares a table before you.

> He anoints your head with oil;
> your cup overflows.
> Surely His goodness and love will follow you
> all the days of your life,
> and you will dwell in the house of the Lord
> forever.

>> Only if you believe.
>> Only if you are adopted.

A bottle of water is pretty interesting.
The only thing that changes its value is its location.

Where are you sitting?

table talk

If you are willing, try this prayer:

Jesus, I believe in You. I choose to believe. Help me with my unbelief. I believe you are the Son of God who died on the cross for my sins and rose from the dead on the third day. Thank you for bearing my sins and giving me the gift of adoption and abundant life. Would you show Yourself to me today and this week. I want to see and hear You. I sign the adoption papers. I believe I am adopted.

If you have prayed this prayer, sign your name here by the prayer along with today's date as a reminder that you have been adopted.

X _____

Expect to see God, your Father, today.

you are invited.

There is a common phrase in our culture that teachers call an idiom:

to bring (something) to the table.

For example:

1) He brings years of leadership experience to the table.

2) When you're writing your resume, you need to make sure you highlight what great things you'll be bringing to the table.

It means to provide or offer a useful skill or attribute to a shared task, activity, or endeavor. Now, I don't know about you, but all this table talk has me thinking about what I can bring to it.

I knew a guy.

I thought he was pretty cool.

I invited him to be part of a leadership team at my church.

He disregarded it.

He said, "I have nothing to bring to the table."

Boy, was he wrong.

After a time of twisting his arm[145] to join, he went on to lead hundreds of people to Christ through his story.

In our world, when we are invited, we automatically think, *What can I bring?* There is a human desire to bring something to the table. Whether it be through skills, abilities, gifts, or even a plate of food, we love to feel like we *earned* the invitation.

But at this table, Jesus says to just bring you.

Nothing else.

Just you.

In your brokenness,

in your weakness.

Come to me, all you who are weary and burdened, and I will give you rest.[146]

-Jesus

He just says come: come to me, come to my table.

I just want you. Even if you have nothing. *Especially* if you have nothing. Especially if you are weak and tired. Don't bring anything, just yourself. You are seen, you are enough, you are worthy, and you are

---

[145] Another fun idiom, one possibly originating from a big brother.
[146] Matthew 11:28.

now my child.[147] Don't bring a thing; I'll take care of the rest. You are invited.

The Psalmist wrote:

He prepares a table before you.[148]

"Prepares" is a word that deems consideration. "Prepares" isn't just a last minute "I threw this meal together" kind of thing. The term signifies time, effort, and thought. He did this for the Psalmist, He does this for me, and He does this for you. He delights in preparing a table with you in mind, knowing that you will bring nothing extra—it's not needed; He just wants you to take a seat.

There is a chair
    somewhere
        with a little place card that has your
        name on it.
            It is pulled up to a spiritual
            table, where you are invited
            to believe and to sit.

***

As a kid, you knew you'd made it when you were invited to a birthday party. Do you remember what it was like, getting a sealed envelope with your name on it? Or how about when others got one, but you didn't?

    At the Lord's table, you are invited.

---

[147] Imagine me requiring my five-year-old daughter to bring something to breakfast to be able to eat.
[148] Psalm 23:5.

I remember being a new kid at the middle school I went to. My middle school years were some of the most awkward years of my life.[149] I didn't have but three friends in an eight-hundred-person school. But, being an athlete, I got to know some cool kids fast. One day, the starting quarterback—a big shot on the team and the cool, popular kid—called my house.[150] He asked if I wanted to go on a trip with him and his parents to San Diego. I, being this new, lonely middle schooler, felt so honored.

Why would he choose me?
was the first thought that crossed my mind.
What do I have to bring to the table? was the second.

But I went.
I was chosen and invited.[151]

This started the beginning of a great friendship, and I found that we became pals based on who we were rather than what we brought to the table.

***

There is this scene in the scriptures where Jesus takes his closest friends and disciples to share a meal celebrating a holiday called "Passover." Passover was a Jewish holiday

---

[149] Mmm-hmm. Trying to figure out life, we all were.
[150] This was before cell phones. People would call the house and politely ask who they would like to speak with as your little sister listened in from the other room.
[151] His other friends probably couldn't go, but it didn't matter. I was still the chosen one.

celebrating a past event where the spirit of death *passed over* the Israelite houses with blood on the doorframe. It is a day to remember when the Israelites were slaves in Egypt and the Lord freed them with Moses.[152] Jews often celebrate by eating together with friends and family.

The time of Passover came, and with it, there was a notable scene:

> *Jesus sent Peter and John, saying, "Go and make preparations for us to eat the Passover."*
>
> *"Where do you want us to prepare for it?" they asked. He replied, "As you enter the city, a man carrying a jar of water will meet you. Follow him to the house that he enters, and say to the owner of the house, 'The Teacher asks: Where is the guest room, where I may eat the Passover with my disciples?' He will show you a large room upstairs, all furnished. Make preparations there." They left and found things just as Jesus had told them. So they prepared the Passover.*[153]

Jesus, being a Jew, wanted to celebrate this holiday with His disciples. He asks Peter and John to prepare a table in some pre-chosen place. When it came time to celebrate Passover, Jesus was ready to party. It's unclear whether they knew the man they spoke to or if Jesus simply invited

---

[152] For more on Passover, check out Exodus 12.
[153] Luke 22:7–13.

Himself.[154] It was a certain man, a nobody—probably just a clueless dude who ended up hosting one of the most pivotal events in the history of mankind. Let me give you a glance at the timeline: This is hours before Jesus is arrested and killed.

The upper room is where many significant events happened in scripture. Here are a few notable moments:
- It's where the famous scene of Jesus washing His disciples' feet took place.
- This is where Jesus famously says, "I am the way, the truth, and the life; nobody goes to the Father except through me."
- Also, it's the same evening that Jesus promises the Holy Spirit will be sent to His followers after He is gone.

This single evening has so many teaching points packed into it. It was like the most incredible night in the history of the world! Can you imagine being there that night? I mean, we teach and preach events from this one evening about 75% of the time in our churches.[155] No wonder Da Vinci's work, *The Last Supper*, is one of the most famous paintings ever.[156]

Back to the scene: They are reclining and eating at this table. Incredible events and teachings are taking place, but what intrigues me the most are the guests sitting around Jesus. Let's take note of who was in attendance that evening—who was *invited* to this significant table. Now,

---

[154] Oh, Jesus. He knows how to party.

[155] I wonder how accurate that stat is. I totally made it up.

[156] Though, the table they were sitting at was probably not a huge, long table with everyone sitting on one side. They were probably sitting in a circle at a small wooden table on the ground.

oddly enough, the guy who was carrying water and owned the house didn't seem to be there.[157] But the disciples of Jesus (Peter, Andrew, James, John, Mathew, Philip, Thomas, Bartholomew, James, Jude, Simon, and, yes, Judas) were present. The closest to Jesus were at the table. His circle. His friends, His brothers, and also the ones who messed up big time.

This was the last meal Jesus would ever have on Earth. You know the question, "If you had one day to live, what would you do?" This was literally Jesus' final days on Earth, and He understood that.

He knew it and chose it.

Imagine the urgency that He spoke with. Imagine knowing that your time has come, and you desperately want to get information to your family and friends before it's too late. He specifically invited the ones he wanted to celebrate and speak with to dinner. The people invited to this table had an important role, but there are two that really fascinate me—Judas and Peter.

Judas was at the table. Judas, the man infamous for being a sellout, gave Jesus up to the authorities for some bills. His name is synonymous with hypocrisy and evil. Judas' feet were washed, and Judas was sitting *at the table*. Jesus knew what was about to happen.[158] Yet, in His knowledge, he had still invited Judas to the table to feast, wash his feet, love, and receive some crucial information.

---

[157] Maybe he had Passover plans at the in-laws?
[158] A little awkward for Judas, if I do say so myself.

Peter was also at the table. Peter walked on water, proclaimed Jesus the Messiah, and was one of Jesus' most devout followers, but he failed when it mattered. At that dinner, Jesus called him out, saying,

> *I tell you, Peter, the rooster will not crow this day until you deny three times that you know me.*[159]

Moments after this meal, moments after Jesus washes Peter's feet, he denies Jesus three times in a row.
      These two were invited to the table.
            Judas and Peter.

Why do I bring this up, you ask? To take a moment to recognize the importance of who was and who is invited to the table. The closest to Jesus. His circle. His friends, his brothers,
      but also the ones who messed up.
           They were at the table.

They were invited to take part in this incredible evening. They were not perfect—far from it—but they sat with Jesus. Peter and Judas had their feet washed, and they participated in the last supper (the first-ever communion) moments before the biggest regrets of their lives.

I don't know you, and I don't know what you have done. I don't know where or how you have messed up. I don't know what you struggle with. I don't know if you even believe in Jesus. I don't know if you have sold Jesus out or plan to.

---

[159] Luke 22:34.

But I do know this: you are invited to the table.

I believe that today you are seen for everything, good and bad. Today you are enough and you are chosen to be adopted, even despite your past and future mess-ups. Today, the ball is in your court.

***

I once went to a different church than the one I usually go to. I sat down and listened to the songs and the teaching of the day, and then something very interesting happened. They proceeded to take communion, a traditional passing of bread and wine, but something strange happened.
They passed the bread around the congregation.
Nobody touched it.
They passed the wine around to the people,
and no one took a sip.

Not one person.

From my own church tradition, I was accustomed to seeing somebody jump on stage and explain communion before we would partake.[160] After all, it is a form of declaration—a symbol to remember Jesus. These services almost always refer to this moment in scripture:

> *On the night He was betrayed, Jesus took bread, and when he had given thanks, he broke it and said, "This is my body, which is for you; do this*

---

[160] Most protestant church traditions occur about once a month, and it's usually a little grape juice and some sort of bread.

> in remembrance of me." In the same way, after supper he took the cup, saying, "This cup is the new covenant in my blood; do this, whenever you drink it, in remembrance of me."[161]

But this particular day, sitting in the pews of this particular church, nobody touched it. It was an event that I will never forget. When the plate came to me, I passed it on. Out of sheer surprise, I did not partake; I did not want to disrupt the service and make a scene. I sat there, and I wondered why. Why did they pass the plates? Why did they not partake? Was this a dream?

I asked some of the congregants about it after the service. This was the answer: Only those who are worthy are allowed to eat the bread and drink the cup. This congregation believed that they were not part of the 144,000 chosen ones discussed in Revelation.[162] To them, it was an act of humility. They thought they were not worthy, chosen, or adopted.

Every bone in my body wanted to scream at the top of my lungs.

> This was not the good news I had come to know and experience through Jesus Christ!

---

[161] 1 Corinthians 11:23-25.
[162] Revelation 7:1-8.

> *This righteousness is given through faith in Jesus Christ to all who believe. There is no difference between Jew and Gentile.*[163]

All who believe.

This is the good news.

In ancient times, there was a big social and cultural difference between the Jews and the Gentiles. Yet, in the above passage, the writer noted zero contrast. This statement would have raised eyebrows back in the day. For starters, a "Jew" was anyone who belonged to God's chosen ones of the twelve tribes of Israel, while a "Gentile" was everyone else. The term was typically used in the Gospels to mean "non-Jewish" or "non-chosen."
But that's not the gospel of the table—the gospel of Jesus Christ.

The non-chosen became chosen. The uninvited became invited. There was no difference then. The great qualifier and equalizer is faith.
You may not be Jewish.
    You may not be an Israelite.
        You may be flawed.
        You may be broken.

            But if you have faith in Jesus Christ, righteousness is given, and it doesn't matter who you are or what you have done; you are invited to partake!

---

[163] Romans 3:22.

I will not mention the church or the people involved by name, but I will say this:

> We are *all* invited to God's table.

Communion is a simple tradition that carries a loaded message. Jesus simply said, "Do this." He didn't ask for your resume first. He didn't keep any invitations to himself. Communion means "common union," and the common union between all of us is that we have all messed up, yet we are still invited.

I invite you to believe that Christ is the Son of God, and that He died as a sacrifice so that all who believe in Him would be saved from sin. When Jesus was sitting in that upper room with His buddies, He said,

"Every time you do this, do it in remembrance of me."

> Every time you sit at a table to eat and drink,
>
> remember me.

It was simply a meal. The wine and the bread were nothing special. It was just a moment they shared a common union, and Jesus took this moment not only for the good ones, but Peter and Judas, too. They were not excluded from the table. Jesus' love for His disciples includes everybody.

> Even us.

How Many Chairs Can Fit at the Table?

Humans often wonder, *How much and how many?* We get stuck in a view that automatically wonders if the seats are numbered and the spots are limited. This has been defined in psychology as "scarcity thinking:" the idea that resources, opportunities, and rewards are limited or scarce, and it's a dog-eat-dog kind of world where you have to take what you need before it's gone.

    An example of this is thinking that a table could only fit so many chairs.

But scarcity thinking is not for the kingdom of Jesus.

The kingdom of heaven is abundant, not limited.

One of the key verses of this book is that Jesus came to give life...

    ...*life more abundantly.*[164]

Abundance means "plenty, more than enough, unlimited." Jesus came to Earth to give us that kind of life. This does not only represent the time after we die. We are invited to an abundant life now, and that abundant life is at the table.

    There is a conversation in the animated movie *The Boss Baby* that illustrates this point well.[165] The plot is about an only child who is deeply loved before he has a baby brother. Then, the new baby begins to receive all the attention and love. The writers and directors do an excellent job of painting this picture of children wrestling over their parents' love. The title is *The Boss Baby* because the film makes it so that winning the love is the mission of this highly intelligent baby voiced by Alec Baldwin. The baby explains to the new big brother that there is only enough love to go around once, and the

---

[164] John 10:10.

[165] I am a sucker for a good kid's movie.

baby gets it all. The baby uses the illustration of beads on a wire; he takes a bead and says, "This is Mom and Dad's love. Before I came, you had all of the beads, but now that I am here, we get to share." But the baby goes on to explain that because he is the baby, new and cute, he actually gets all the beads. The baby gets all of the love. This is often the way we, as humans, view love. We have to share it, and one day, it will run out.

This is not the love of God. There are enough beads, enough love, and enough chairs to go around.

It says that God loved the world so much that *whoever* believes gets the gift.

> *For God so loved the world that he gave his one and only Son, that whoever believes in him shall not perish but have eternal life.*[166]

God's love isn't shared—it is limitless.
> There is more than enough to go around. God's love is real, steadfast, and unchanging.

When my wife and I had our first child, I experienced love like never before. I fell deeply in love with my daughter. When we were about to have our second child, one of my fears was that I wouldn't have it in me to love another child as much as the first. I was worried that I would have a favorite, and my second child would be second in love. This was not the case. Instantly, I found that not only did I have enough love to go

---

[166] John 3:16.

around, but it felt like the love grew and grew and overflowed into my children.[167]

You are seen, you are chosen, you are adopted, and you are invited to sit.
Yes, you. God's table grows, and there are always plenty of seats. And, by the way, there's one with your name on it.

***

One of my favorite scenes in the Bible occurs after Jesus dies.

According to scripture, Jesus came back to life and began to visit many people, but there is a moment when he shows up to Peter that is breathtaking. Remember, this is the same Peter who denied Jesus three times.

"I'm going out to fish," Simon Peter told them...
> He is probably sulking, feeling guilty and ashamed.

...and the others said, "We'll go with you."
> Because that's what friends do.

> *So they went out and got into the boat, but that night they caught nothing.*
> *Early in the morning, Jesus stood on the shore, but the disciples did not realize that it was Jesus. He called out to them, "Friends, haven't you any fish?"*
> *"No," they answered.*

---

[167] I love them equally, but make no mistake, it is not in the same way. My love for each of my kids looks very different. You can't love any two people in the exact same way. Hmm, I wonder what God lessons we can take from that?

> He said, "Throw your net on the right side of the boat, and you will find some." When they did, they were unable to haul the net in because of the large number of fish.
> Then the disciple whom Jesus loved said to Peter, "It is the Lord!" As soon as Simon Peter heard him say, "It is the Lord," he wrapped his outer garment around him (for he had taken it off) and jumped into the water. The other disciples followed in the boat, towing the net full of fish, for they were not far from shore, about a hundred yards. When they landed, they saw a fire of burning coals there with fish on it, and some bread.
> Jesus said to them, "Bring some of the fish you have just caught." So Simon Peter climbed back into the boat and dragged the net ashore. It was full of large fish, 153, but even with so many the net was not torn. Jesus said to them, "Come and have breakfast."[168]

When Jesus calls out, "Friends, have you caught any fish?" our English translation doesn't do it justice. Can I nerd out for a moment?

> The original Greek word typically used for a friend was *philos* (φίλος), but the word used in this sentence is *paidion* (παιδίον).

---

[168] John 21:3–7.

Here is this word as described by Strong's Lexicon:[169]

Paidion (παιδίον)
a young child, a little boy, a little girl

1. *infants*
2. *children, little ones*
3. *an infant*

Jesus wasn't just calling his "friends." He was calling his adopted children. He was calling his kids back from their guilt and shame. Calling them to Him and His abundant life.

Lastly, he calls them to breakfast. He leads them to the abundant catch of fish. Then He says, "Come and eat. Come and enjoy the gift."
You may have received the gift of the fish, but it's not until you come to Him that you get to eat.

Receiving the gift of abundant life from God is one thing, but it's another to actually open and use the gift. To sit at the table.

It's kind of like getting a gift on Christmas morning, looking to the gift giver and saying, "Thank you," then putting it right back under the tree to walk away and get back to your things.

No. You open the gift, and you experience it.

---

[169] *Strong's Concordance* provides an index to the Bible of its Hebrew and Greek words. This allows the reader to find words where they appear in the Bible. It also lets the reader see how the same word may be used elsewhere in the Bible. I love to use the free online study tool called blueletterbible.org, myself.

***

God's table is huge. He has a seat for every single person in the world. But there are a lot of empty seats—probably even dusty ones. Why? Because a lot of people have yet to hear this invitation of abundant life and others still believe the invitation is for later in life. Or, like many of us assume, they believe it is not for our time on Earth.

But the abundant life is for the here and the now.
The table is for you.

There are two types of people in this world: those who are scrounging the streets for food and those who are sitting at the King's table.

Step one in getting to the table is putting your faith and trust in Jesus. In other words, you must sign the adoption papers and accept the free gift of God. But that's not all.

Second, we have to realize who we are and simply respond to the invitation—we sit. That's it.

You must understand that we have been seen, recognized, chosen, adopted, and so we sit at the table to receive and enjoy abundant life.

As a kid, you know you've made it when you are invited to a birthday party. But you still need to actually go to the party. That's where all the pizza, games, and cake are.

This is the table.

I am the gate; whoever enters through me will be saved. He will come in and find <u>pasture</u>.[170]

> *He makes me lie down in green <u>pastures</u>,*
> *he leads me beside quiet waters,*
> *He refreshes my soul.*[171]

The thief comes only to steal and kill and destroy; I have come <u>that they may have life, and have it abundantly</u>.[172]

> *You prepare a table before me in the presence of my enemies. You anoint my head with oil;*
> *my cup overflows.*
> *Surely <u>your goodness and love will follow me</u>*
> *<u>all the days of my life,</u>*
> *and I will dwell in the house of the Lord*
> *forever.*

Do you see it?
    He prepares a table before you.
        Your invitation is waiting.
            The only thing you need to bring to the table is you.

---

[170] John 10:9.
[171] Psalm 23:2-3.
[172] John 10:10.

table talk

Let's do communion together.

Sit (physically sit) at a table with some food and a drink. Visualize yourself enjoying the presence of Jesus there with you, at the table.
When you eat, remember Him and all He has done for you. When you drink, understand the sacrifice He gave you. Practice every day eating in remembrance of Jesus Christ.

Pray this, if you would:
> *Lord, I am willing. I am sitting here at your table.*
> *Help me receive your gift of abundant life*
> *right now.*
> *Amen.*

> Now, expect it.
> Blessings, my friend.

Here I am! I stand at the door and knock. If anyone hears my voice and opens the door, I will come in and eat with that person, and they with me.

– Jesus of Nazareth
Revelation 3:20

part two
now what?

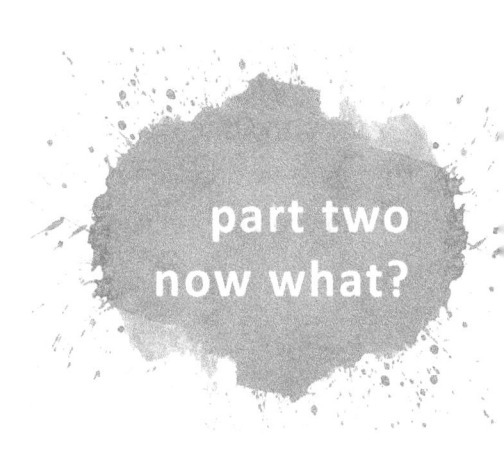

Imagine with me for just a moment
        that you are at the table.

    You sat down.
        You begin to look around at the scenery,
        wondering what's about to happen.

You take a deep breath; your lungs fill with fresh air—pure oxygen.

        Minutes seem like seconds.
          Time stands still.

For the first time in a long time, you think and feel so clearly.
        It's an almost meditative state.

You become incredibly aware.
    You notice personal fatigue.
        You realize your body and feet are weary, but now they are at rest.

There is a sense that you have arrived, yet more is to come.
        An anticipation looms within you.

You begin to ponder your feelings when the lights start to dim, and three beings step into the room: God the Father, God the Son, and God the Holy Spirit. They arrive, and they sit next to you, surrounding you.

> Peace and joy fill the air.

The table is massive, and there are others there, but you feel as if you are the only one in their presence. You are overwhelmed by a serenity that you have never felt before. They exude an unexplainable presence. You begin to worship—effortlessly.

> They look at you and you feel like never before: seen, worthy, wanted, and honored.
>
> But you soon realize there's more.

You notice your body ache and your stomach growl. You're hungry, and you feel an impossible appetite rise up in you. There is a craving that you have deep in your soul; you've felt it before, but never this strong. Your body is in dire need of food, but not just any old hamburger will do. You body wants a different type of food—a spiritual food. For whatever reason, an excitement begins to build.

Your senses magnify.

Music emerges softly and slowly.
Soon, you realize that it is a playlist of your favorite songs. Then, like ice skaters, God's heavenly waiters and waitresses come gliding in, carrying dishes and bowls of the most magnificent-smelling foods your nose has ever processed.

They begin to place the plates on the table. The food is sumptuous; it includes everything from your all-time favorite grandma's enchiladas to the most unique and colorful dishes your imagination could comprehend.

> Your body is drawn to the food.

You begin to look around in amazement. You whisper under your breath, "Is this all for me?" They look at you in unison and say, "Of course, my child." God the Father tenderly looks into your eyes and says, "Thank you for joining us. We have been eagerly waiting for you. Let's eat!"

> From the first taste to the very last spoonful, every taste bud on your tongue is screaming for more. You are eating and eating. You have never had food this good. It is perfect. The bread is soft and doughy, the vegetables are fresh and crisp, and the meat is so tender it cuts like hot butter. The food seems like it never depletes. You are not full, but you are fully content.
>
> You are simply eating because of the ease and because of the joy.

Then, they begin to talk.

They share how much you mean to them and how much they love you. They start speaking to you about some of your favorite topics: your family, your school, your work, your favorite sports team—everything you love to talk about. At first, you were nervous to speak because you realized you were speaking to God, the creator of all, the King of kings; yet, you've organically found yourself deep in conversation. And for so long, you have heard about this "relationship" we can have with God, but you have had yet to experience it like this. This is not the God you grew up believing He was. He is not old with a great, long, white beard and holding a list of all of your wrongdoings. He is loving and exudes peace. The three of them together create perfect harmony, and the unexplainable three-in-one somehow makes sense. The Father, Jesus, and the Holy Spirit act as one, yet they are all very different in expression.

Normally, talking doesn't come the easiest to you, but you realize this is one of the most effortless conversations you have ever had. It's like talking to your best friends, mom, grandpa, or favorite teacher. It's even like speaking to yourself in another body—natural and easy. Every question that you planned to ask God is forgotten, but the conversation flows so smoothly that you feel like you are being enlightened and encouraged anyway, and God seems to be answering all the questions you never knew you had. You realize this is not an interview or an interrogation and not a time where God scolds you for messing up and lists all the bad things you have done. It's easy. It's glorious. It's full of love. You never want to leave.

You then notice others at the table.
Other people are experiencing the same thing as you. Organically, relationships and discussions begin across and throughout the table. The conversation and time with

the table.

the others at the table is fulfilling for everyone. There is no agenda, no stress, no intimidation… just pure connection. It's therapeutic.

But then, Jesus looks at you and says, "I have something for you. A plan. A mission. A purpose."

He hands you something. It's a gift. You open it up to find a mirror, but when you look into it, you notice something different about your face. A good difference: You are swathed in confidence, peace, and joy. You then notice the presence of God in your eyes and all around you. God is behind and in front of you as well as to the right and to the left of you. The presence of God is on you, and you see it and feel it.

Then, God the Father touches your cheek like a loving dad and the Holy Spirit flows into you. Your heart begins to ache for your family, neighbors, and community who are not at the table. People and issues back in reality begin to come to mind. You are beginning to see things the way God sees them. Your heart is breaking for the same things that break God's heart. Instantly, fear and sadness engulf you.

> But then you glance at Jesus. You begin to be inspired by creative thoughts and actions.
>
> There is a confidence and a peace stronger than your human emotions.

Your gaze falls back to God the Father, and the stress begins to fade. He says, "You know what to do, and you have what it takes. Where you go, We will go with you...

...always."

Full of purpose, you stand up.

***

You've made it to part two of this journey.
I know your time is precious and limited, so I will get to the point.
I believe God's table has three primary functions for those who sit:
1. You eat.
2. You connect.
3. You share.

Let's jump in. But first, let me pray for us:
God the Father, Jesus, and Holy Spirit. We are here at the table, in your presence. Show us the wonders of Your great love. Lead us and guide our mind as we read. We are open to seeing, feeling, and experiencing things we never thought possible.

Amen.

you eat.

"Let food be thy medicine and medicine be thy food."
— Hippocrates

"People who love to eat are always the best people."
— Julia Child

"Tell me what you eat, and I will tell you what you are."
— Brillat-Savarin

Food is a commonality that we all share.

Every culture has prioritized food and exemplified creativity and art through cuisine. Whether you are in my home state of California or across the world in the beautiful country of Burkina Faso, food is food.[173]

Our world is full of diverse people, thoughts, styles, interests, and food, but one unifying factor between us all is that everybody needs some sort of nourishment. Food provides this.

---

[173] California is home to some of the best food in the world. What makes it the best? The diversity, variety, and excellence.

In the 1950s, after the Korean War ended, South Korea was left with a large number of children who had been orphaned by the war. As a result, relief agencies came in to deal with all the problems that arose with having so many orphan children. One problem they encountered with the children in the orphanages had to do with their sleep. Even though the children had three meals a day provided for them, they were restless at night because they had great anxiety about whether they would have food the next day or not. To help resolve this problem, the relief workers in one particular orphanage decided that each night when the children were put to bed, the nurses would place a piece of bread in each child's hand. The bread wasn't intended to be eaten; it was simply meant to be held by the children as they went to sleep. It was like a security blanket for them, reminding them there would be provision for their daily needs. Sure enough, the bread calmed the children's anxieties and helped them sleep.

> Food is important.
>
> It's a need in everyone's life. Without the consistent intake of food in our lives, we become weak, ill, and challenged.[174]

Whether it's a home-cooked meal, a trip through the drive-thru, or a five-course dinner at a fine dining restaurant, food nourishes, fuels, and gives people satisfaction.

I happen to love food.

---

[174] And grouchy... Don't forget grouchy.

I say that as if some people don't. Most people like food. It's one of those things in life you kind of have to do. Yet, some people take it to the extreme—like me. One of my hobbies is eating. I love trying new restaurants and new foods. I travel to new places just to try new grub. We have this term for radicals like me: "foodie." A foodie is pretty much someone who devotes their life to finding a variety of good food.

Everybody in their own right is a foodie because with it comes life. Here is a simple graphic:

$$food = life^{175}$$

To further the point. Most doctors and trainers would also argue:

$$good\ food = better\ life$$
$$bad\ food = worse\ life$$

There is so much truth to the phrase, "You are what you eat." Why is it that when I am having a tough day or suffering from some low-grade depression, all I want is junk food? I reach for the tub of ice cream.[176] I told you I am a donut lover, but do you know how to make me not want a donut? Offer one to me after a great workout. It's the last thing I want; my body craves something different.
Something healthy.
My family and I recently watched the 2004 documentary "Supersize Me" by Morgan Spurlock, and an interesting experiment takes place within it. He eats only McDonald's for

---

[175] I wanted this to feel like a textbook, so I had to add this complicated graphic.

[176] No need for a bowl; I'll just eat it with a spoon.

thirty days, and the transformation in his physical body and mentality is alarming.[177]

I wonder how many of us are what we eat.

May I make it spiritual?
Rob Bell[178] has faced some healthy criticism lately, but I appreciate his view that everything is spiritual,
> because it is.

>> How many of us have a constant spiritual diet of cheap fast food? How many of us are starved for something a little more spiritually substantial?

>>> I am convinced many of us are spiritual foodies. Even those of us who have nothing to do with church, religion, or God.

We are constantly searching and looking for the next best thing. Why have people always been drawn to religion, a spiritual cause, or a deeper meaning? It's because we were built to have a spiritual diet as well as a physical one. This

---

[177] It was traumatic for my kids, who love Happy Meals.

[178] Rob Bell is a writer and speaker who once pastored the fastest-growing church in America. TIME magazine thought he was a big deal in 2011, naming him one of the world's most influential people. Some of his writings and teachings have come under scrutiny from the mainstream Christian church. A documentary about him, *The Heretic*, came out in 2018. However you view the man, he is an incredibly creative communicator.

the table.

is often found in mystics, theology, cults, and meditation. Something deeper, something more, something spiritual—it is part of the human appetite. Our body becomes weak, ill, and challenged without a steady flow of something real.

> Something from the Lord's table.

We, as a human race, were built to eat: physically and spiritually.

> What are you eating... spiritually?
> Stop and ask yourself this for a moment. Even spend some time in thought with this question: What does your spiritual diet consist of?

Maybe you're thinking of the last time you went to church or read the Bible. It's much deeper than that.

It's something that only this spiritual table presents. God's table offers us what we need to not only survive but thrive here on Earth. The table provides us the abundant life.

There is a really important and famous scene where Jesus' closest disciples ask him how to pray. Prayer is one of those things: Nearly everyone knows what it is, but hardly anyone thinks they know how to do it.[179]

So they saw an opportunity, and they asked,

> *"Lord, teach us to pray, just as John taught his disciples."*
> *He (Jesus) said to them, "When you pray, say:*

---

[179] Don't worry, you're not the only one who gets a little nervous when asked to pray.

> *'Father, hallowed be your name,*
> *Your kingdom come.*
> *Give us each day our daily bread.'*[180]

The disciples probably have seen Jesus pray over and over again in their time with him, and this is the moment they finally humbled themselves enough to ask Him to teach them. They hated walking with the Lord but not knowing what they were doing when it came to praying.[181]

Jesus teaches them this world-famous prayer, and he adds this request:

> *Give us each day our daily bread.*

If Jesus prayed about bread and said that this was the model, then eating is a pretty big deal. It can also be noted that there is a bread that comes from the Lord, our Father. Now, you can explain it by saying, "Yes, God made the grains that man uses to bake bread," but I suggest it's more profound than that. When Jesus said to pray this line, there was both physical and spiritual intent to that prayer. We cannot live without physical food for nourishment, nor can we live spiritually if we do not have Christ in our lives every day. It is the first moment in the prayer that Jesus requests something for himself. This means when it comes to asking, food is priority number one.

***

---

[180] Luke 11:1-4.

[181] But like most men, it's sometimes hard to ask for directions.

There is this scene from the scriptures that is pretty radical. It's after Jesus fed five thousand people with some fish and some bread. After Jesus does this miracle, according to John, he vanishes for a day from the crowd. It's implied that the crowd began looking for Him and when they found Him the next day, Jesus said,

> *Very truly I tell you, you are looking for me, not because you saw the signs I performed but because you ate the loaves and had your fill. Do not work for food that spoils, but for food that endures to eternal life, which the Son of Man will give you. For on Him, God the Father has placed his seal of approval.*[182]

Did you catch that?

Food that endures to eternal life...

> When you eat the Lord's bread, it leads to eternal life and it endures.

A moment later, Jesus says,

> *For the bread of God is the bread that comes down from heaven and gives life to the world.*[183]

This bread that Jesus is speaking of gives life to the world.

> An abundant life.

Then finally, the kicker:

---

[182] John 6:26-27.
[183] John 6:33.

> *Jesus declared, "I am the bread of life. Whoever comes to me will never go hungry, and whoever believes in me will never be thirsty."*[184]

***

One of my favorite things to do is to go out to a restaurant to eat. I find so much joy in choosing what I want, having someone prepare it for me, and not cleaning up.[185] And I must say, one of the best feelings in the world is sitting in a restaurant, patiently and hungrily waiting for your food to arrive, and then watching the waiter or waitress bring your food through the kitchen door. They walk straight to your table, sit the plate down in front of your face, and ask if you need anything else.
You reply, "Nope," and go to town.

There is really something special about eating. The action not only nourishes our body, but it is delightful to eat. Yes, food is fuel for our bodies, but it's not as if we are just "fueling up." Cars do that. As humans, we *enjoy* the fueling!

Food is one of God's love languages, and I think this is why the average human has about 10,000 taste buds—and, get this, they get replaced about every two weeks for fuller, fresher tastes.[186] My only response is that God is good, and He loves us. Like, *really* loves us. God could have made everything taste the same. Even something great like the

---

[184] John 6:35.

[185] I know, I know. I am a spoiled brat sometimes.

[186] Teachers know these random facts. It's what we are taught in Teacher School.

combo of chocolate and peanut butter would be great for like half a day before we'd get tired of it. I thank God for food because food is good—especially Asian food![187]

There is an ancient prayer of the Christian church that says, "Blessed are you, Oh Lord God, King of the Universe, for you give us food to sustain our lives and make our hearts glad." Food definitely makes my heart glad!

Throughout scripture, there is a sense that food, or bread, is a symbol of blessing. Here are some examples from Scripture:

> *I have heard the grumbling of the Israelites. Tell them, "At twilight, you will eat meat, and in the morning you will be filled with bread. Then you will know that I am the LORD your God."*[188]

- Once they eat the food, they will then know that God is Lord.

> *He gives food to every creature. His love endures forever.*[189]

- He gives food as an outpouring of His love.

> *He upholds the cause of the oppressed and gives food to the hungry, the LORD sets prisoners free.*[190]

---

[187] My favorite.
[188] Exodus 16:12.
[189] Psalm 136:25.
[190] Psalm 146:7.

- In the same sentence as the oppressed being set free is a mention of food.

The biblical image of food I suggest today is that eating symbolizes blessings in life. In fact, in the not-so-ancient past, being overweight was a sign of wealth and prosperity.

Food nourishes and gives strength and energy. But as we have discussed, it's more than just physical.

I really like this translation and interpretation of John 6 from The Message Bible by Eugene Peterson:

> "The real significance is not that Moses gave the bread from heaven but that my Father is right now offering you bread from heaven, the real bread. The Bread of God came down out of heaven and is giving life to the world."[191]
>
> - Jesus

When I was heavily exercising in the gym two times a day through college, skipping breakfast was a definite no. We knew, as athletes, that food intake was an important part of growth and health—especially concerning the *right* food. During my time playing with the university baseball team, we had two-a-days, which were days where we would work out before the sun came up and then go to class and then report

---

[191] John 6:23-33 from The Message Bible.

the table.

back to the field later that day; these were extreme days for the body. But one day, I woke up a little later than I usually did. I popped up from my pillow and urgently looked at the time.[192] I jumped out of bed and ran to practice, skipping my morning bite. I ended up making it on time, but I missed my essential morning nutrition before our workout. We then had a rough training, of course.

We were not halfway through the workout when I began to feel nauseated. I remember doing some sort of squat and blacking out. When I woke up, I vomited on the ground.[193] The first question the team trainer asked was about what I had for breakfast. He gave me a granola bar and a banana, and I felt like a new man.

I do not have to go into this lengthy convincing argument that food intake is essential; I take it you understand. Yet, even in scripture, eating spiritual food is discussed at length. Paul speaks to drinking spiritual milk and moving our way to spiritual steak and potatoes. My daughter loved milk as a baby, but if she never graduated to solid food, I am pretty sure she would not be the healthy, beautiful girl she is today. There is something about eating the right kind of food. Eating diverse types of food is important and necessary for physical growth and health, just as eating spiritual food is vital for spiritual growth and health. That is what is offered at the table.

---

[192] Every human knows the feeling of sleeping in a little bit and frantically looking at the clock. It's the worst.

[193] Eww.

You may be sitting there reading and thinking to yourself, *Yep, Dave, that sounds good and all, but how do we eat invisible food at an invisible table?* You may be a little worried about my sanity or fearful that I will simply leave it there.

Give me a chance to explain.

In the following few lines, I plan to break down a few ways to eat that have led to an abundant life for me. Again, I haven't fully made it, and there are days when I am in the dumps.

I'm not some spiritually special guy and I am not a know-it-all, but I have tasted and I have seen the abundant life.[194]

I am still learning, asking the Lord to show me His table, His food, and the abundant life He promised. It is a journey, but it's worth it.

For me, I've eaten at the table and experienced a fuller life through a few disciplines. I want to break down the word "discipline." Typically, when we hear the word, we often think of Dad taking off his belt.[195] Discipline is often used to describe a consequence of a negative action, but I want to assure you that this word has a glorious meaning behind it. "Discipline" comes from *discipulus*, the Latin word for "pupil" that also provides the source of the word "disciple." Think of

---

[194] Psalm 34:8.
[195] I might get in trouble for saying that nowadays.

the table.

it this way: discipline is like a trellis in which grapevines grow. Without the trellis, the vines go crazy, but with the guide, the plant flourishes. If you are a disciple, disciplines are part of the way of life.

And, in my experience, the way to eat at the table.

I want to let you into some of my personal disciplines, which have helped me grow. I have seen personal transformation as I have "eaten" through these disciplines. Now remember, any discipline (whether it be school, weightlifting, healthy eating, or learning that new skill of juggling) takes effort, work, and consistency to learn. I promise you, it is so very easy to get caught up in doing something for a few days and then getting tired of it and quitting. But please stop doing that. Lebron James did not become "the king" just by showing up; he put in the work.[196] He spent tireless hours training his body, his hands, and his brain to do what he wanted it to do on the court. He was disciplined. In the same way, in order to eat the full buffet meal, in order to become the best version of yourself, and in order to experience the abundant life, you must be disciplined.

I'd like to challenge you with the law of twenty-one. Twenty-one days, that is. Any time we commit to something, we must give it twenty-one days.[197] Once you get to the end

---

[196] Okay, don't freak out. While Lebron may be "King James," MJ is still the GOAT.

[197] Twenty-one days in a row, or three weeks—whichever one you think sounds better. It's brain science.

of the twenty-one days, you can decide whether or not to move forward.

With anything that you commit to taking on, know that you will go through four phases:
1. The honeymoon
2. The fight through (part one, physical)
3. The fight through (part two, mental)
4. The injection

Let me explain.

In the beginning of January, gyms across America are filled with people who have resolved to get into shape. Gyms are full of excited people wearing headbands and their new gym shoes. Hence, we enter phase one. As you know, the honeymoon phase will tell you this is easy, and you are going to be fired up on whatever you are doing. You will probably find joy in what you're doing for the first few days. Don't assume that you are a natural; this is normal. At the beginning of January, everyone believes they are gym rats. But by January 10th, people begin to fall away.

Enter phase two. The first fight phase is tough. It's physical. Your inspiration and beginner's love fade, and reality steps in. You are tired. You don't have time, and your pain is convincing. You must fight past comfort and not hit the snooze button. You are overcoming your physical wants.

Then, the next fight comes around. This phase is the toughest; it's the mental fight. The third phase will try to mentally convince you that you don't need it anymore. This is after you have been working out for three weeks and have yet to see any results. Your brain will try to get you to think that it's not worth it. While the physical fight is simply pushing past physical boundaries, the second fight is internal. You have been praying for a while, and now you are getting bored and feel like it's not working. Fight, my friend; get through the growing pains. By January 20th, hundreds of thousands of people will fail to win the fight. They will give in and quit working out. But not you.

The last phase I call the injection, because once you get through the fights, whatever you are trying to do becomes almost second nature to you. It is injected into your bloodstream. It becomes your routine. My friends, when you get there with healthy spirit disciplines, it is a glorious feeling. There are certain people whose exercise habits are woven into their routine and it is natural for them. These are the people who develop. If you get to phase four with some of these "eating" disciplines, that is where the real tasting and feasting begins.

Now, I only want to spend a little bit of time here because this is not a book on disciplines; there are already plenty of good writings about that.[198] But for the sake of eating and experiencing the abundant life, disciplines are how you get there.

The Discipline of Reading and Writing

One time, Jesus was approached by the devil himself. Jesus was hungry, and the devil offered him bread.

---

[198] If you are interested in reading more about some spiritual disciplines, you've got to check out my guy Richard Foster.

Jesus responded,

> *Man shall not live on bread alone, but on every word that comes from the mouth of God.*[199]

> Bread is good, but the words of God are better. It satisfies our soul's hunger. We get to eat and live off of every word that comes from God. The most straightforward way to do that is to make a daily routine of personal Bible reading.

This is something that, without a doubt, has been one of my most incredible growing tools. I read every day. Sometimes a few chapters, sometimes a few lines, but I read and ask God to guide my understanding. I then journal how God is speaking to me. There are so many plans and ways to read the Bible out there, so I will just share one that is my bread and butter.[200] Find a consistent reading plan, or just read a book in the Bible chapter by chapter. I recommend starting with Luke. Luke was a physician whose sole purpose was to share the story of Jesus with his friend Theophilus. It's written in a no-nonsense style that makes understanding Jesus the goal.[201]

And it's not enough to just read the "daily bread;" I like to write a little bit, too.[202] Journaling is another discipline that takes cognitive processes and moves them to the physical

---

[199] Matthew 4:4.

[200] Bread and butter... I guess I am sticking with that food analogy.

[201] When you are done with Luke, move on to the book of Acts. Luke wrote that one as well, outlining how a believer should act and respond.

[202] I've always understood that guys call them journals while gals call them diaries. Is that really a thing?

activity of handwriting. It's good for brain science. Find a journaling strategy that fits your style, but for the sake of sharing, here is my favorite: the acronym SHAPE.[203]

Scripture: Start by reading your sections of the Bible for the day. Mark in your Bible and highlight, underline, or star the verses that speak to you. Then write out one or two of them in your journal.

Hear: Next, take time to hear from God. What does He have to say about this verse or verses? Really, spend some time asking the Lord what it means for your unique life. As you practice listening, He will become clearer and more accessible. Write down what you believe the Lord is speaking to your heart. Write it out in the voice of God. When we read the Bible, it is God's divine word; expect God to speak to us.

Apply: Now, we move to the part where the rubber meets the road. We apply what we have read and heard to our life. Write down an action or two that you could put in place today.

Pray: It is good to seal this commitment in prayer to God. Take some time to write a prayer to God about what is on your heart. Thank God for the words, then ask Him to help you, encourage you, and strengthen you to follow through on your commitments and desires for the day.

---

[203] Thank you Mountain View Church of Clovis, CA. You guys will forever have a place in my heart for being so foundational for me as a disciple.

Exalt: We want to take time each day to praise God and be thankful for the blessings we have received.

Reading the Bible is the initial way to position yourself to receive and eat the spiritual food at the table. It's the first step in grabbing your fork and knife and digging into the abundant life Jesus has for us.

The Discipline of Memorization

A friend of mine keeps a handful of 3x5 cards with scripture written on them everywhere he goes. Every morning, the first thing he does is review the cards. He takes time to internalize them, day after day. So much so that these passages become part of who he is. Memorizing scripture renews our mind and transforms our life.

There is a passage in Deuteronomy that says,

> *Fix these words of mine in your hearts and minds; tie them as symbols on your hands and bind them on your foreheads.*[204]

When engulfed with scripture, it becomes part of who we are. Our mind is being pressure-washed to holiness.

For me, the easiest way to memorize scripture is to read it repeatedly. Don't make it complicated. I also know there are some more sophisticated and fantastic ways to aid in memorization that you can find on your phone.[205] Try reading

---

[204] Deuteronomy 11:18.
[205] There's an app for that.

a verse ten times daily until you've memorized the whole thing. Repetition tends to have a staying effect; the more frequently you internalize it, the more solidly it will root itself in your mind and heart.

Where to start? Take a meaningful verse to you and commit to it. Try it for twenty-one days straight. Dr. Greg Smalley of Focus on the Family suggests ten verses every Christ follower should know:

- John 3:16
  For God so loved the world that he gave His one and only Son, that whoever believes in Him shall not perish but have eternal life.

- Jeremiah 29:11
  "For I know the plans I have for you," declares the LORD, "plans to prosper you and not to harm you, plans to give you hope and a future."

- Philippians 4:13
  I can do everything through Him who gives me strength.

- Romans 8:28
  And we know that in all things God works for the good of those who love Him, who have been called according to His purpose.

- Proverbs 3:5-6
  Trust in the LORD with all your heart and lean not on your own understanding. In all your ways acknowledge him, and he will make your paths straight.

- 1 Corinthians 13:4-7
  Love is patient, love is kind. It does not envy, it does not boast, it is not proud. It does not dishonor others, it is not self-seeking, it is not easily angered, it keeps no record of wrongs. Love does not delight in evil but rejoices with the truth. It always protects, always trusts, always hopes, always perseveres.

- Romans 12:2
  Do not conform any longer to the pattern of this world, but be transformed by the renewing of your mind. Then you will be able to test and approve what God's will is—His good, pleasing and perfect will.

- Philippians 4:6
  Do not be anxious about anything, but in everything, by prayer and petition, with thanksgiving, present your requests to God.

- Joshua 1:9
  Have I not commanded you? Be strong and courageous. Do not be afraid; do not be discouraged, for the Lord your God will be with you wherever you go.

Lastly, our themed verse:

- Psalm 23

    The Lord is my shepherd, I lack nothing. He makes me lie down in green pastures, he leads me beside quiet waters, he refreshes my soul. He guides me along the right paths for his name's sake. Even though I walk through the darkest valley, I will fear no evil, for you are with me; your rod and your staff, they comfort me. You prepare a table before me in the presence of my enemies. You anoint my head with oil; my cup overflows. Surely your goodness and love will follow me all the days of my life, and I will dwell in the house of the Lord forever.

The Discipline of Withholding

This one is fascinating.

>I am about to say an oxymoron,
>>which means that it contradicts itself.

>How do you eat at the Lord's table? You don't eat for a period of time at your table.
>>It's called fasting.

Although Jesus or the Bible never directly commands this, examples of fasting appear in both the Old and New Testaments. One of the most revealing passages about it is when fasting is mentioned by Jesus in Matthew 6:16. He is speaking to His disciples on the basic principles of godly living, and when speaking on fasting, He begins with, "*When* you fast," not "*if* you fast."

> Jesus' words suggest that fasting should be a regular discipline and routine in His followers' lives.

Maybe you've skipped meals to lose weight or been too busy or tired to cook before, but that's not fasting.[206] Fasting isn't some magic ceremony to get God to answer our prayers and give us abundant life. Remember, we don't earn our spot at the table, and we don't earn an abundant life. We are *given* it. Fasting is about what we gain from the process: It's a focus on our time at His table.

It was actually during Jesus' fast that He quoted Deuteronomy and said, "It is written: 'Man shall not live on bread alone, but on every word that comes from the mouth of God.'"[207] Fasting helps us understand the reality of our spiritual appetite. We receive a better understanding that Jesus is the bread of life who nourishes us and provides abundance.

When I was living in Africa, I was awestruck that there was a group of believers who—living on minimal food—chose to fast one day a week. When I was with them, I was always so hungry because their eating schedule and routine was minimal compared to my American habits. I couldn't imagine giving up meals in Africa; it was unthought

---

[206] Ha! Good try, oh holy one.
[207] Matthew 4:4.

of. Yet, the abundant life they experienced and the beauty that came from understanding their spiritual appetite was magnetic. I remember thinking that if they could do it, I could certainly do it. Fasting has since been inserted as a weekly practice for me and my life. I know there are other things to "fast," like sweets, television, or social media, but I like to keep food as the focus because of what it represents.

Here are some practical fasting tips from our brothers and sisters at NewSpring Church:[208]

1. Start slow. If you've never fasted before, begin with just one meal.
2. Continue to drink water to stay hydrated. While some individuals in the Bible fasted from both food and water, this choice can be dangerous if you're not experienced with fasting or haven't consulted a medical professional.
3. Don't overeat before or after your fast. Eat smaller, healthier meals, including raw foods, before and after.
4. Tell only people you must, but try to be considerate of others in your schedule if you fast.
5. Consciously reflect on scripture and your experience. Your physical response will often reveal spiritual truths.

The Discipline of an Abundant Life Mindset

This leads us to the promise of abundant life. Let me start with this: an abundant life doesn't mean that life is perfect and you are now rolling around in a Rolls Royce with your

---

[208] NewSpring Church in South Dakota.

stunna shades on. The life of the one who sits at the table is challenging. Yet, let me suggest it as a discipline.

Living an abundant life means focusing on the blessings in your life rather than focusing on what has been taken away or is lacking. Living in abundance does not mean you have an abundance of things. Material possessions are momentary; they are here today and gone tomorrow.

> *Do not lay up for yourselves treasures on earth, where moth and rust destroy and where thieves break in and steal, but lay up for yourselves treasures in heaven, where neither moth nor rust destroys and where thieves do not break in and steal. For where your treasure is, there your heart will be also.*[209]

Speaking of food, God assures us that we do not need to worry about what we will eat or what we will wear. While physical things are blessings and gifts from God, neither riches nor poverty are indications of whether one is sitting at the table and experiencing an abundant life or not.[210]

> Authentic abundant living comes from an inner peace, joy, and gratitude toward life. We must be grateful for what we have, not wishing for or pursuing what the world argues we need.

For a disciple of Jesus, fullness of life is not measured in terms of wealth, power, or prestige, but by seeking God and His goodness.

---

[209] Matthew 6:19-21.

[210] Like what our culture wants us to believe.

To live an abundant life, we must be disciplined enough to change our mindset. Focusing on what we have rather than what we want is a mindset shift. This is not natural for human beings. As noted earlier, we are wired to compare ourselves with others, and usually, we don't see ourselves or what we have in a positive light. We are wired to be selfish and greedy. This is a direct attack against the discipline of abundant living.

> Your mental saboteurs are constantly going to be scheming to get you to believe bad things about yourself or your things as often as they can.

Gratitude journals have been a buzzword lately, even in the secular world. This is a step towards living an abundant life.

> Try it.
> As quickly as you can, list ten things you are grateful for in your life right now.

What happened? Did you notice the mindset shift? Was it easy?
Was it challenging?
You may have thought of things such as:
- Your health
- The roof you have over your head
- Your job
- Your family
- The food you have to eat
- The sun shining

- Being alive
- Having a good friend

I challenge you to keep a running list. Add to it over time. Whenever you find yourself wishing for something you don't have, seek out the positive.

An abundant life consists of an abundance of love, joy, peace, patience, kindness, generosity, faithfulness, gentleness, and self-control; it is no coincidence that these are metaphors of food as well in the Bible—often referred to as the fruit of the spirit.[211]

An abundant life is promised to the disciples of Jesus as not necessarily a place to go when you die, but something available now—something we can experience here on Earth today. An abundant, full, best life is not only some sort of future happening, it is available now.

According to scripture, if you follow Jesus, you are promised eternal life and (as us humans refer to it) will go to heaven. But God also wants to play a part in your life right now, while you're here on Earth.

It's an abundance of life, not stuff.

Jeremiah 29:11 is one of the most often-quoted verses in the Bible. I have come to believe it represents our time at the table. It represents God's love for us and our lives. It represents abundance.

---

[211] Galatians 5:22-23. More on that later.

> *"For I know the plans I have for you," declares the Lord, "plans to prosper you and not to harm you, plans to give you a hope and a future."*[212]

God has a desire for you to succeed in life and to live abundantly. He wants you to eat at his table and prosper in all things; your family, your relationships, your health, your finances. Yet, if we don't feed our spiritual appetite, our soul does not prosper. Nor will other areas of our lives.

Living an abundant life means declaring that we genuinely believe in God's goodness and providence. Abundant living means believing God is working for our good. Anything we lack, God has in abundance. We have everything we need in Him. Our view of God, the table, the food, and this life will determine our view of abundance.

Here are some scriptural reminders of spiritual food:

- *Set your minds on things above, not on earthly things. For you died, and your life is now hidden with Christ in God.*

  – Colossians 3:2-3

- *Every good and perfect gift is from above, coming down from the Father of the heavenly lights, who does not change like shifting shadows.*

  – James 1:17

---

[212] Jeremiah 29:11.

> - *Now may the God of hope fill you with all joy and peace in believing that you may abound in hope by the power of the Holy Spirit.*
>   – Romans 15:13
> - *And my God shall supply all your needs according to His riches in glory by Christ Jesus.*
>   – Philippians 4:19

***

So, my friend, I challenge you: *eat.*
Life is too short to sit at the table and stare at the food in front of you.[213]

Remember, eating is a choice, and it is on you.
Nobody, not even the Lord, will come do the choo-choo train and feed you.

> You have to make a decision to feed your spiritual appetite, stay committed, and enjoy the abundant life at the table.
>
> Bon appetit.

---

[213] Yikes, talk about hell on Earth.

table talk

What do you want to eat?
Seriously.

What is something that you want to add to your life? A discipline that you wouldn't mind putting on your plate?

An abundant life is offered to you as a free gift. But just because it's free, doesn't mean it's easy.

Let me pray this over you.
As you read these words, receive them deep in your soul.

Father, in the name of your Son Jesus, and in the Power of your Holy Spirit, I declare feasting over the one who reads these words. May they come to know You and Your abundant life today. Right now.

Help them Lord, guide them, and give them the desire to be disciplined at Your table.

Amen.

Eat today, my friend.

you connect.

"Food brings us together, and at its best, it's a form of love."
– Alice Waters

"There is no sincerer love than the love of food. Unless you're talking about the love of food shared with friends and family, which is even better."
– Unknown

"My idea of heaven is a great big baked potato and someone to share it with."
– Oprah Winfrey

I love this story that Jennifer Rothchild[214] shares:

> Rose was an elderly widow who lived nearby. Many of us college students regularly visited her to check in on her.
>
> One evening, my friend, Mike, popped in at dinner time, and Rose invited him in. They visited for a few moments... that is, until Mike noticed her kitchen table was set for two.

---

[214] Jennifer is an American author, speaker, podcast host, and the founder of Fresh Grounded Faith events for women. She's pretty legit.

"Oh, Rose," he said, "I didn't realize you were having a guest over for dinner. I will scoot out."

She stopped him and explained that ever since her husband died over thirty years earlier, she always set two places at her table. Mike assumed the second place setting was to remind her of her late husband and thought about how sweet that was.

But Rose corrected him.

"Oh, no," she shared, "I set a place at my table every evening for Jesus. I sit with Him, listen to Him, and expect Him to be with me."

***

Sharing tables is one of the most uniquely human things we do. No other creature sits and consumes its food at a table.[215] But tables are more than just for eating. Sharing tables with others reminds us that there's more to the table than just fueling the body.

Think about the last time you shared a meal with someone else at a table. Did you just put your head down and feast?[216] Most likely not. We don't sit at a table just to eat;

---

[215] Imagine if a cheetah chased down a gazelle, tackled it (National Geographic style), and instead of tearing into it, it put a napkin around his neck, pulled a chair to a table, grabbed a knife and fork, and delicately started slicing and eating his catch with his good friend named Charles.

[216] Well, it depends...

we hang out, play games, take it easy, cool down, create, learn, unwind, and connect with others.

This is a primary purpose for our time at God's table.
> To simply be with Him,
>> and Him to be with us.
>>> To build a relationship.

After moving out and getting married, my parents started doing something pretty cool: They would host us for dinner once a week. It was nice because we didn't have to cook or even pay for anything;[217] we just had to show up. We would simply eat and talk—that's it. Our relationships grew in a matter of time. My wife began to truly see my parents as hers. My dad became a fatherly voice in her life. Her relationship with my parents grew stronger than it ever had. Even my relationship with them drastically changed.

This became an important staple in the family because of the relationship-building that came along with it.

As I've gotten older, I learned this:

> Without intentional time together, life flies by. If you do not make use of it, life will pass without truly connecting with those around you.

There is a saying that says, "A family that eats together stays together." The truth stands not in the meatloaf and mashed potatoes, but in the proximity with others.

The time together.

---

[217] Free is always good to some happy-go-lucky newlyweds who are not making too much money.

> As humans, we were built for relationships. Deep, meaningful connections.

When I want to get to know someone, I invite them to eat with me.[218] It's usually through a meal that I learn about a person. In some ways, a table disarms us; in some ways, we lay down our weapons and armor to eat, giving us the opportunity and the vulnerability to talk. In ancient medieval times, banquets and mealtimes between opposing kings and countries would be a time of peace and reconciliation. It's in humility that humans recognize our mutual need for food.
Humility creates space for connection.

***

When I first started getting to know my wife, I would take her on dates.[219] These dates would usually revolve around some sort of activity, but they would always end or begin with sitting around a table for a bite to eat or a drink to drink. Why do people date? So that we can get to know each other.[220]

> Sharing a meal together is a handshake. It's a relational practice. It's a "look me in the eyes" kind of interaction.

---

[218] I'm buying.

[219] Trying my best to be romantic and sweep her off her feet. I guess it worked. 😊

[220] We would go see a movie occasionally, but we did not prefer it because we didn't get to talk. We would finish a two-and-a-half-hour movie and not learn one thing about each other. There is a time and a place for movies and hand-holding, but it is nothing compared to a face-to-face conversation.

This is what makes sharing a meal with God so interesting because, in some ways, it is God's way of connecting with us. He invites us to the table for *us* to get to know *Him*—He already knows everything about us.

> There are times for holding God's hand, but His genuine desire is that you would talk and walk with Him. He wants you to get to know Him.

***

In ancient times when dealing with God (or gods), sacrificing was a common and called-upon practice. In the midst of this ancient sacrificing world, a prophet named Micah says,

> *With what shall I come before the Lord and bow down before the exalted God?*
> *Shall I come before him with burnt offerings, with calves a year old?*
> *Will the Lord be pleased with thousands of rams, with ten thousand rivers of olive oil?*
> *Shall I offer my firstborn for my transgression, the fruit of my body for the sin of my soul?*
>
> *He has shown you, O mortal, what is good. And what does the Lord require of you?*
>
> *To act justly and to love mercy, and to walk humbly with your God.*[221]

---

[221] Micah 6:6-8.

To walk humbly, to me, means to walk alongside. To walk humbly with God is get to know God. More than any sacrifice, God desires to walk with you, to sit with you, and to connect with you.

Isn't that something? In an ancient world where sacrifice was the religious norm, the requirement to walk humbly with a god would have been an outrageous thing to say or believe.

But this is the God we serve.

Not a God who needs you, but one that wants you.[222]

> Read that above line one more time.
> Nice and slow.

The Bible describes God as a loving father. A God who knows how many hairs we have on our heads; who knows our past, present, and even our future. This is a God who knows everything about us, and what He desires is for you to get to know Him. Jesus repeatedly said, "If you know me, then you know my Father." There was an urge to know God. When Jesus taught his disciples to pray, he didn't start with "Oh, mighty God," or "Dear holy creator." No, He taught his disciples to say,

> *Our Father...*[223]

---

[222] It's nice to be needed, but you're not really needed by God. He's God—He can totally do what He wants. Read that again, He doesn't need you, He *wants* you.

[223] Mark 6:9.

The first line of that prayer is an invitation to know God intimately, and it's deeper than a creator/creation relationship.

It's a father/child kind of thing.

> This is what makes the God of the scriptures so intriguing to so many—He actually cares about us.

In no other religious faith does the God of the universe, the creator of all, the King of kings, want so significantly to know you and be known by you. In no other faith-based belief does their "god" pursue the people. In no other world does the king sit with the peasants and the poor at His table. No other god wants to have breakfast, lunch, and dinner with you.

But this King does.

This God loves you so much that He wants to spend time with you. He wants to know you and wants you to know Him.

> He pursues you, He chases you, and He desires you.
>> Not because of what you have done, but because of who you are.

This was made clear when I was on a journey through my studies to get my degree in Bible and religion. When studying the scriptures in this fashion, one can often be tempted to treat the readings as a textbook. But I found the more I studied scripture, the closer I wanted to know this guy named Jesus. One of my early prayers that prompted my faith was a simple sentence:

"Lord, help me get to know You."

This prayer was revolutionary with my experience at the table.

All too often, we get so caught up in going to church, reading our Bible, praying, tithing, and being good that we lose sight of the heart of our Father: to simply be in His presence. Sure, God loves us so much that He plans to make us better; He truly wants to make you holy rather than just happy. But let's not overlook the truth that God doesn't want or need anything from us; He simply wants us to be with Him.

King David had it right when he penned these words:

As the deer pants for streams of water, so my soul pants for you, my God. My soul thirsts for God, for the living God.
When can I go and meet with God?[224]

Some translations even close the passage with "When can I be in the presence of God?"

How beautiful, right?

---

[224] Psalm 42:1-2.

> Every parent's dream is for their kids to want to be with them.
>
> Especially when they are grown and making their own decisions.
>
> This is the heavenly Father.

Love Letters

I have heard the scriptures described as letters to us. Imagine getting a letter from your spouse and treating it like an article you found in the newspaper. It's not to be studied as a text, it is intended to be read with emotion.[225]

When my wife and I started dating (and even now) we would leave love letters for each other hidden in different spots. When I received one, I would often read it over and over again. I would cherish it.

It was never like, "Oh, I don't have time to read it," or "Man, I just get so bored reading that stuff," or "I just don't get it, so I quit reading," which, if you have noticed, are all common excuses that we use when talking about reading the Bible.

Let's think of the Bible as His love letters to us. The truth is that God wants you, and He wants you to get to know Him. Once you get to know Him, your life changes. Sometimes gradually and sometimes instantly. God does what He wants, but He is in the transformation business. As we get to know

---

[225] Unless the letter is to take out the trash or to pick up the dog poop. Then that's a totally different kind of letter. I'm talking about a love letter.

God, our lives organically become better. Have you heard the phrase, "You become the average of your five closest friends"? This is true, by the way, but imagine if Jesus was one that you spent most of your time with.[226] We do not do good things to become holy and closer to God; we do good things because we *are* holy and growing closer to God.[227]

As I am writing this, we just passed another Father's Day. It was glorious. My kids made me little homemade cards with sketches and words about me. They are both developing their fine motor skills, so the drawings are... We will just say cute. The words are scribble lines. But when they bring me their cards, they are glowing with excitement. They quickly tell me what the drawings are and what the words say. It is always so very beautiful and hilarious at the same time. As the Father's Day gifts continue to come through the years, I would hope to continue to get little cards and presents (hoping their fine motor skills continue to develop), but as they grow older, their childlike innocence may fade. The cards may turn into store-bought ones, and I might start getting ties as presents instead, but I will always cherish these things from my children.

But can I say this?

I don't need that stuff.

> What I really love and desire is when my kids simply crawl into my arms and read me their notes. I treasure the moment, the time together, much more than the gifts.

---

[226] Our average would greatly increase, obviously.

[227] You may need to read this again; it's a bit of a tongue twister.

Don't get this mixed up. A lot of people's view of God is more like a pawn shop owner than a loving father. Like, you get things when you earn it. But let me redefine that relationship. As you read these lines, read a little slower, because this is important.

> God simply wants you and wants you to know Him. As you sit at the table, understand that you were invited to eat and, more importantly, to build a relationship with God.

How does one develop a relationship with God?
Well, how do you get to know a friend? You hang out with them, you talk with them, you listen to them.
The same is true with God.

Reading the love letters He left for us gives you time with your Father.

Talking to Dad

Often when we hear the word "prayer," our brains automatically tune to something: something we've been taught, something we've seen on TV, something we've learned from our grandma. In other words, there is baggage when it comes to that word.

> But let me say this:
> > Prayer is simple.
> > > It's easy, and it's natural.
> > > > Quit overthinking it.

> Prayer is a discipline of
> getting to know God.

I love this line from the scriptures:

> *Rejoice always, pray without ceasing, give thanks in all circumstances; for this is the will of God in Christ Jesus for you.*[228]

The writer wouldn't have said "pray without ceasing" if it wasn't possible.
Prayer is more than just folding your hands and closing your eyes. Prayer is deeper than getting on your knees by your bed.

> Prayer is a way of being.
> It's as simple as breathing.

Prayer is communicating with the creator of the universe. What an incredible privilege! What has often been modeled to us is that these "talks" with God turn into a list of things we want and then finish with an awkward… "That's it. Amen."

I want to remind you that any conversation is two-way.[229] God wants to speak, too. Next time you pray, place an empty chair in front of you and imagine Jesus sitting there.[230] Once you imagine Him sitting there, just start talking. But then—oh, this is the best part—ask Him to speak to you and pray that you would have ears to hear.

---

[228] 1 Thessalonians 5:16-18.

[229] Unless you're speaking to a wall.

[230] He can look however you want Him to look.

Then listen.

Actually listen.

It feels weird at first, but God will lead your thoughts. He will give you pictures or visions, and He will speak to you.

My sheep hear my voice, and I know them, and they follow me.[231]

Nothing else will satisfy your deep longings.

Not marriage.

Not a child.

Not riches.

Not the perfect body.

Not that car.

Not that dream vacation.

Not retirement.

Not anything.

Nothing but God.

Only God.

But wait, there's more.

The connection doesn't stop there.

Sitting at the table means you are sitting with a new family.

Fellowship

Think for a moment about the people and the relationships you are surrounded with. Our lives are constantly enriched by family, friends, and acquaintances.

---

[231] John 10:27.

Beyond that, many of us have hundreds of other connections in the virtual world of social media.

It's argued that relationships are the most essential aspect of our lives,

> and it's true.

The people that surround us are the ones we become.
> Fellowship is important.
> And fellowship is another gift of sitting at the table.
> To connect with others who are also living an abundant life.

Have you ever visited an old church with a fellowship hall? It's usually this room near the front where donuts and coffee live. It was a place where people could do some small talk and engage in "fellowship" before church started.[232]

I appreciate the heart behind naming it that, but may I suggest something? Biblically, fellowship is referred to as a noun rather than a verb. Meaning we don't go do fellowship; we *are* a fellowship.

Acts 2:42-47 describes the first believers who, in contrast to their individualistic society, "devoted themselves to the apostles' teaching and the fellowship, to the breaking of bread and the prayers."

> This is a definition of what it means to sit at the table; it requires devotion and fellowship.

---

[232] I am using a bunch of air quotes because, as I write it, it sounds so silly.

In the words of Kyle Idleman,[233] God and his people have many fans, but devotion requires one to be a fanatic.

In a world where personal success and self-focus take center stage, the idea of fellowship in the Bible offers a different path. Before you start thinking I am some cult leader,[234] see for yourself—these verses aren't just lines to read, they're friendly invites to dive into deeper relationships, promote togetherness, and live out a faith that transforms (kind of like how the early Christian church did).

> John 17:21
> *That they (believers) may all be one, just as you, Father, are in me, and I in you, that they also may be in us, so that the world may believe that you have sent me.*
>
> 1 Corinthians 1:9
> *God is faithful, by whom you were called into the fellowship of his Son, Jesus Christ our Lord.*
>
> 1 John 1:7
> *But if we walk in the light, as he is in the light, we have fellowship with one another, and the blood of Jesus his Son cleanses us from all sin.*

---

[233] Kyle is the pastor of a pretty big church in Kentucky. On a normal weekend, he speaks to more than twenty-five thousand people across eleven campuses. He is also the author of one of my favorite books, *Not a Fan*. Check it out.

[234] One time, someone told me I'd make a great cult leader. I don't know whether to be offended, worried, or flattered.

Acts 4:32

Now the full number of those who believed were of one heart and soul, and no one said that any of the things that belonged to him was his own, but they had everything in common.

2 Corinthians 6:14

Do not be unequally yoked with unbelievers. For what partnership has righteousness with lawlessness? Or what fellowship has light with darkness?

Ecclesiastes 4:9-12

Two are better than one, because they have a good reward for their toil. For if they fall, one will lift up his fellow. But woe to him who is alone when he falls and has not another to lift him up! Again, if two lie together, they keep warm, but how can one keep warm alone? And though a man might prevail against one who is alone, two will withstand him—a threefold cord is not quickly broken.

These passages remind us of how important it is to connect with others at the table among us in the Christian faith. These lines encourage us to build strong bonds like the early believers in Jerusalem did. Yes, it's okay to have friends outside of the faith, but the abundant life comes from looking across the table and saying, "Oh, you too?"

Let's Get Practical

In a world where everyone focuses on themselves, we're asked to live differently by connecting with others at the table and experiencing God and His abundant life together. Let's not just think about these verses, but let them push us to live out this new way of connecting.

Step One: Find a Church Home

"I like Jesus, but I'm not a fan of going to church."

"I don't want those church people who act one way and say another telling me how to follow God."

"My connection with God is personal; I don't need others telling me how to worship."

I've heard plenty of folks make statements like these. Most likely, they've been hurt by their experiences with the church, viewing the community of believers more as a source of pain than of support. They've felt wounded by those who claim to understand God's grace and forgiveness. It's a deep hurt when such pain comes from a close relationship.

You probably know people like this, or you might even feel this way yourself. If this hits home for you or someone you know, take a moment to reconsider your perspective on the church, which is often referred to as the bride of Christ.

Access to good teachings is as easy as a few clicks these days. You can listen to the best preachers and teachers our world offers, but that's not church. That's not the abundant life of fellowship Jesus promised. Church is about being connected.

I know of a church that stopped live-streaming its services. Sure, they lost some of their financial givers, but they found that the live-streaming made room for people to isolate.[235] I commend them for that decision. That's not who we've been called to be at the table.
Find a local group of people headed the same direction as you. No, they're not perfect. Yes, the church can be flawed.
But you are called to fellowship despite that.
And remember, you are human too.

Here is a simple five-step process for someone who is a Jesus follower to find the right church:

1. Seek Recommendations: Ask for recommendations from fellow followers of Jesus, friends, or family members. They can provide insights into welcoming church communities.

2. Visit Multiple Churches: Attend services at different churches in your area. Pay attention to the atmosphere, teachings, and community spirit.

3. Engage with Leadership: Reach out to the church's pastor or leaders to discuss your questions and learn more about the church's beliefs and mission. Are they aligned with the teachings of Jesus and the Bible?

---

[235] Why get all dolled up to go somewhere when I can just stay home in my jammies and watch from my couch, Fruity Pebbles in hand?

4. Participate in Church Events: Attend church events, Bible studies, or community gatherings to gauge your comfort level and fit with the people.

5. Pray and Reflect: Take time to pray and reflect on your experiences, seeking guidance from your faith or a higher power. Make a decision based on your observations and discernment. Let the Lord lead.

There is no perfect church, but it's vital that you join others running in the same direction as you. These five steps should help you find the right community that aligns with biblical beliefs and provides a supportive and fulfilling fellowship. But remember, it will take you diving in to get there.

Step Two: Get to Know the People Who Are Sitting at the Table

As our culture has become more engulfed in technology and social media platforms, we have begun to lose the ability to actually connect. Sure, we are masters at surface-level small talk, but what I am talking about is real, authentic conversation.

I am not downing tech at all; I love my technology. My life functions more efficiently because of it.[236] But there is another side to it. I promise you, when we are sitting at the spiritual table of God, nobody is scrolling on their phone.

---

[236] Thanks, Alexa!

I don't know about you, but having a conversation has always been a little awkward with some people. While some discussion happens naturally, many of us never learned how to actually do it. So we do what's comfortable and revert to small talk. This prevents meaningful relationships from forming.

I once attended a workshop that taught, step by step, the route to conversation. It's strange and a little robotic initially, but I share this today because it has helped me in many ways.

Next time you meet someone new, keep these mental images and associations in your brain:[237]

- Nametag
    - First up, the name tag represents what your name is. Ask what their name is.
- Boot
    - The name tag is stuck on a boot, which represents work. What does this person do for work?
- Home Plate
    - The boot is placed on a home plate in a baseball stadium. This represents home. Where are they originally from? Where do they live?
- Crowd
    - The home plate is in a stadium that is full of people. This represents family and friends. Who are they? Where does the family live?

---

[237] These might sound a bit weird, so don't get all judgy on me, but I promise they've actually worked for yours truly. Give 'em a whirl next time you meet someone new.

- Airplane
    - As you look up, an airplane is flying overhead. This represents traveling. Where do they like to travel?
- Tennis Racket
    - Oddly enough, the propeller on this plain is a tennis racket. This represents hobbies. What do they like to do for fun?
- Light Bulb
    - In between the netting and the handle on the racket, there is a lightbulb. The lightbulb represents ideas. What are some ideas or dreams that this person has? What are they passionate about?
- Private First Class (PFC) Soldier
    - The PFC soldier is screwing in this lightbulb, and he represents what **p**roblems, **f**ears, and **c**hallenges they may have concerning their dreams and ideas.
- Field Goal Post
    - On top of the soldier's hat stands a field goal post. This represents the goal of conversation: to get to a point when you begin talking about their heart for Christ and His purpose in their life.

Now, that's weird, isn't it? But this systematic recipe for conversation has been a great tool for me as I engage and connect with others. I'm not saying you go in order or hit every step—hardly. This is simply an outline that, if you can memorize, is a tool to have something to talk about.

Remember, sitting at this spiritual table may be your future best friend, spouse, co-minister, your next mentor, collaborator, or your next eager student, waiting to be discovered. Discovery always starts with a listening ear and a good conversation.

***

Tables are for food, but also for relationships.
Imagine the table as a symbol of connection, and not just any connection, but a connection with God and with those around you.
Think about it: You can have your own personal journey with God and see your relationship with Him flourish, but there's something profound about being part of a community and coming together as the church. It's woven into our very nature, deep in our DNA—the need for a tribe or a group to belong to.

That's where the magic of the table comes alive. It's more than just a piece of spiritual furniture. It's a place where connections are fostered and nurtured. It's a reminder that, in the heart of God and of His table, we find that sense of true belonging.

> So pull up a chair. The table is where connections spark and relationships begin.

table talk

This is two parts.

Part one:
Put a chair in front of you. Have a conversation with God as if he was your friend. Tell him the things that are on your heart. Visualize him. Listen to Him.

Part two:
Go to church. Meet some people. Engage in conversation. Join a small group.

Begin asking the Lord, who in your life needs to be in your inner circle.

Pray for a mentor, pray for the right friends, and pray about who you can share your life experiences with.

Then call them. Shoot them a text and have some food with them around a table.

you share.

"We make a living by what we get, but we make a life by what we give."
— Winston Churchill

"A candle loses nothing by lighting another candle."
— James Keller

"Sharing is like a best friend who steals your fries but then shares their dessert with you."
— Unknown

My grandma used to sing me a song. You may know it. If you do, sing with me:

> ♫ Jesus *loves the little children, all the children of the world.*
> *Red and yellow, black and white, they're all precious in His sight,*
> Jesus *loves the little children of the world.*

It's a simple truth, uttered so
frequently that we often fail to truly
grasp its significance, but
Jesus loves you.

He loves you so much.
He loves being with
you, giving you food,
and watching you eat.

But there's more.
I guess you can say He has an agenda.
A kingdom agenda.

Because He loves *all* of us,
not just the ones sitting at the table.
All the little children.

For God so loved the (whole) world that He gave his only Son, that whosoever believes in Him shall not perish but have eternal life.[238]

Everybody has a chance to experience the abundant life.
Everybody has a chance to sit at the table.
Not only that, but God's heart longs
for all to experience His table.

I want you to know there is a deeper purpose to you, my friend. You see, once you accept the invitation to the table, it comes with a task. As you are sitting there enjoying the

---

[238] John 3:16 with emphasis added.

glorious meal with the King, your eyes will begin to see how He sees. Your heart will start to ache for what makes His ache. As you eat and enjoy yourself, you will start to recognize that you are beginning to see and feel what God Himself sees and feels.

Around that table, you will notice many chairs.
You may even see the names of your closest relatives, nearest friends, classmates, and coworkers etched into the seats.

But the chairs are empty and collecting dust.

God-given passion wells up in you. You look at the head of the table. You look at Jesus Himself, and He says,

> *All authority in heaven and on earth has been given to me. Therefore go and make disciples of all nations, baptizing them in the name of the Father and of the Son and of the Holy Spirit, and teaching them to obey everything I have commanded you. And surely I am with you always, to the very end of the age.*[239]

It's called the great commission.
Once you are sitting at the table, the King will commission you.

If we wholeheartedly embrace the teachings of the Bible, we won't be able to ignore the fact that there are people close to us who haven't yet tapped into the fullness of life. Even

---

[239] Matthew 28:18-20.

more unsettling is the realization that they might be on a path toward an eternal hell—a separation from God.
   A separation from the table.

Visualize this scene:
  You are commissioned by the Head of the table.
    You stand up,
     full of purpose,
      full of direction,
       and empowered. You know the Lord is with you,
        and you go back into your reality
         on a mission.

Full-Time Ministry

In today's world, there's an unsaid misconception that "full-time ministry" is merely a job choice—a path exclusively reserved for a select few.
But let me be clear: ministry isn't a career path, it's the pulsating heartbeat of every disciple.

Full-time ministry isn't a profession; it's a way of life for those who sit at the table of abundance. In fact, the most potent evidence of one's commitment to following Jesus is the unmistakable impact of their ministry.

A "calling to ministry" is not a mere occupation switch. Ministry isn't just another nine-to-five gig; it's a relentless calling that should infiltrate every corner of your life. When people approach it like a job change, they miss the whole point and leave a trail of unfulfilled purpose behind.

Think about this:

Does our world today need more career pastors? Or does it need doctors praying over their patients, teachers pastoring their students, police following the leading of our Lord, and lawyers worshiping in spirit and in truth? Our world needs more Christians rising up and taking Christ into their everyday lives.

Don't get me wrong, I am not knocking those who work in the church. I deeply respect those who have dedicated their lives to ministry in the local congregation or as overseas missionaries. It's a beautiful and commendable choice, and it often involves great sacrifice. Some of my closest friends have devoted their work life to the local church, and there is something beautiful about leaving the rest of the world to commit completely to the betterment of the local church. But it's not for everybody, and certainly not what every Christian should aspire to. Even Paul himself, potentially the world's most influential preacher and church planter, was a tentmaker by trade.

This makes these words even more profound:

> *And whatever you do, whether in word or deed, do it all in the name of the Lord Jesus, giving thanks to God the Father through him.*[240]
>
> — Paul

Paul was a tentmaker by trade, but his life was ministry. Whatever he did, he did in the name of Jesus.

---

[240] Colossians 3:17.

Full-time ministry is the calling for every believer.
> That means us, wherever we are at.
>> Whether we work at the mall or drive a truck for a living,
>> whether we find ourselves looking at teeth all day or doing taxes,
>> or whether we are taking orders or giving orders,
>>> our life is our ministry.

If you are sitting at the table, these words are for you:

> ...*Go and make disciples of all nations, baptizing them in the name of the Father and of the Son and of the Holy Spirit, and teaching them to obey everything I have commanded you.*[241]

Imagine our families, neighborhoods, schools, and communities if the people who followed Jesus served him with their lives as ministers, not just churchgoers.

What an incredible charge.
Your task—part of your role—is to invite as many people to the table as you can: making disciples, baptizing, and teaching.

> You, my friend, are called to be a full-time minister
>> wherever you go.

---

[241] Matthew 28.

Food

Isn't it fascinating how, in the Bible, many of the post-resurrection accounts involving Jesus revolve around food?

In the book of Luke, for instance, we find the risen Jesus walking incognito with two of his disciples. It's only when they reach the village of Emmaus and Jesus breaks bread during dinner that they finally realize who He is.

There's another remarkable scene where Jesus appears to a group of disciples and casually asks, "Hey, got anything to eat here?" and they give Him a piece of baked fish (Luke 24:13-48).

It's intriguing how these seemingly ordinary moments of sharing a meal are infused with profound spiritual significance.

Then there is John 21:1-14—one of my favorite scenes in the Bible.

Seven of the disciples decide to go fishing in the Sea of Galilee after the death of Jesus. Then, out of the blue, Jesus shows up after a whole night of fishing and says, "Hey, let's have breakfast!"

What really grabs me in this story is when Jesus simply says, "Come and have breakfast." None of the disciples needed to ask, "Who are you?" They just knew, deep down, that it was the Lord.

But there's more to it.

While eating breakfast on the beach, Jesus has this heart-to-heart with Peter. It's a powerful moment, especially considering Peter's recent denial. The dialogue between Jesus and Peter during this breakfast on the beach is especially intriguing; take a look:

> When they had finished eating, Jesus said to Simon Peter, "Simon son of John, do you love me more than these?"
> "Yes, Lord," he said, "you know that I love you." Jesus said, "Feed my lambs."
> Again Jesus said, "Simon son of John, do you love me?" He answered, "Yes, Lord, you know that I love you." Jesus said, "Take care of my sheep."
> The third time he said to him, "Simon son of John, do you love me?"
> Peter was hurt because Jesus asked him the third time, "Do you love me?" He said, "Lord, you know all things; you know that I love you."
> Jesus said, "Feed my sheep."[242]

This scene takes place after Peter really messed up. He was probably feeling down on himself and full of shame. He probably didn't want to get out of bed in the morning, but here he was. And here was Jesus.

Notice Jesus asks Peter three times.

There has been much commentary on the significance of the three questions, but in some ways, Jesus is giving Peter a chance to recall what had happened. Peter, probably confused by Jesus asking the same question three times,

---
[242] John 21:15-17.

was reminded later of his three denials. But after each response, Jesus charges Peter with a job.

In spite of what happened, the response of Jesus each time is to, in some way, take care of the sheep.

Capable

I recently came across a story about a pair of horses. In the story, after living free and wild, they were confined to a stall for an astonishing three months. They were fed regularly, but no one bothered to clean out their stall or grant them the freedom to roam.

When the stall door was finally opened, one would expect these horses to eagerly dash out and embrace their newfound liberty. However, to everyone's surprise, they refused to budge. These were horses that, just a few months earlier, had reveled in running, chasing, and playing in the pasture. Yet, after being cooped up for so long, they seemed to have forgotten their true nature. They preferred to remain in their soiled stall rather than venture out into the world.

It took a patient process of gradually leading them outside for them to regain their senses and finally leave the barn. Once they caught sight of the open pasture, they galloped through the gates and rediscovered their carefree selves.

People can sometimes find themselves in a similar predicament. Life's challenges can make us lose sight of who we are and what we are capable of. We may start believing that our current circumstances are the best we can hope for, resigning ourselves to a life lacking in hope.

Just as those horses needed a fresh start, the disciples needed encouragement, too. Both our minds and bodies require periodic rejuvenation. This might involve sharing a meal with friends or taking some time in solitude to recharge. Jesus understood that, at that moment, what his disciples needed most was a good meal, some rest, and an opportunity to be refreshed.

Once we have tasted and seen, something Jesus calls us to do is to go. Go and feed others. You've sat, you've eaten; now go and share it with other people. Part of eating at the table is not hoarding it to yourself, but sharing this incredible opportunity with everybody you can. Go and tell others your story, making disciples of Jesus and baptizing them in the name of the Father, the Son, and the Holy Spirit. Invite them to the table to eat the food that has been promised to all. My favorite part of the great commission is the promise that Jesus is with us. The one who has all authority in heaven and on this earth is right by your side.

He calls out to each and every one of us and asks if we love him. If our response is yes, then we have an assignment:
Go and feed the sheep.
Get others to the table.

Work vs. Works

If you have made it this far in this book, it is not new to you that we are invited to sit, to be saved, and experience the promised abundant life through the love and grace of God the creator. This is not due to anything we have done. Hence, we get the ole phrase "saved by grace, not by works" that nearly every Christian had as a bumper sticker or shirt in the 1990s.[243]

Let's be clear, you are saved by grace, but that doesn't mean you just sit around for the rest of your life doing nothing. That's called being lazy. Jesus said, "Go and make disciples." He didn't say sit in church and wait to die. While we are not saved by doing kingdom things, we are commissioned to work for the King of kings.

Check out this short line from the book of Ephesians:
> For we are God's handiwork, created in Christ Jesus to do good works, which God prepared in advance for us to do.[244]

Some translations translate "handiwork" as "a masterpiece." You are created by a creative creator, but it wasn't on the assembly line. You are His work of art. He fashioned you with intentionality, purpose, and effort.

You were created as His masterpiece on purpose, with a purpose.

> We are not saved by our work, but we are saved so that we can work.[245]

But know this: it is not on you. The food, the invitation, the salvation, and the life of those around you are not fully your

---

[243] My youth pastor's favorite shirt. He wore it every Wednesday night.
[244] Ephesians 2:10.
[245] If I was preaching, I'd say that again so that everyone would hear it.

...sponsibility. You were just called to go; go and love. God does all of the heavy lifting.[246] To think that the eternal safety of the world is my responsibility is crazy! Remember, God doesn't call the able, the significant, and the qualified. He calls the willing.

Are you willing?

If you are, try this prayer:

> Lord, whatever You want to do, I am willing. Help me with my unbelief and my abilities. I trust You, and I am Yours. Lead me to others who need You.

Overflow

When I was a kid, I saw a pastor describe our role as Jesus followers like this: He held up a cup and said, "Pretend this is you. Once you become a believer in Jesus and receive who you are, God fills you up." He then took a pitcher of water and filled up the little cup.
Then he said, "Once you are full, you go to other cups, pour into them, and fill others up. When you are empty, you return to God, get filled up again, and repeat."
He looked at the congregation and said, "This is the great commission."

I disagree.[247]

---

[246] You should take a sigh of relief. I know I did.
[247] With due respect. I understand his point, but I still think he is a little bit off.

I guess the illustration makes some sense, but that model is absolutely exhausting. With all respect to that pastor and that illustration, I believe scripture supports a different model. Scriptures shows us a cup that *overflows*.

So, imagine that same cup, but instead of a pitcher of water, imagine a water hose that continually pours into the cup to a point where the water is flowing over the brim and into every area outside of the cup. I believe this is described in the book of John:

> *...but whoever drinks the water I give them will never thirst. Indeed, the water I give them will become in them a spring of water welling up to eternal life.*[248]

That water becomes a spring—a fountain flowing within you.

You see, I believe that once you eat at this table and drink of His cup, you don't have to work, work, work trying to love and be nice and save the lost souls. It is more like the image of an overflowing cup. We just have to be open, willing to be used, and positioned by God.

Let me take you back to a time in my life when things were spinning faster than a whirlwind. I was a full-time teacher in a public school, doubling up as a pastor, happily married with two adorable babies, and smack in the middle of a chaotic house remodel. Stress had become my middle name, and anxiety was my constant companion. You see, I had fallen for the illusion that it was all up to me, and that's a heavy burden to bear. It took a close friend of mine to set

---

[248] John 4:14.

me straight and tell me to relax. He gave me permission to receive rather than just give, give, give.

"God is good, and He's got this."[249]

Imagine a juggler juggling a bunch of stuff in the air. He's doing his absolute best to keep them from crashing down, but here's the kicker about juggling: No matter how skilled you are, sooner or later, something's going to hit the ground. Sadly, I realized that in my frantic juggling act, my number one priority (my precious wife and kids) was the one taking a tumble.

That's when I heard it. A gentle whisper in the midst of the chaos. A still, small voice that said, "David, let me move in you and then through you. This isn't about you, my friend. Let me overflow; let my presence permeate every nook and cranny of your life." It was a wake-up call like no other.

So, I mustered up a simple prayer, "God, I can't do this alone. I need you. I need the Holy Spirit to fill me up and pour out from me." What happened next was nothing short of incredible. It was like a divine floodgate had opened. Suddenly, I felt peace and joy washing over me, and the realization dawned upon me that God wasn't relying solely on me. He then began using me as a personal, handwritten invitation to others.

Every facet of my life began to flourish under the hand of God. It was a beautiful transformation—a reminder that we're not here to carry the world on our shoulders. Instead, we can let God's grace and love flow through us, lighting up our lives and inviting others to join the table of divine abundance.

---

[249] So simple, but so needed.

I saw the reality of the following:

> *You anoint my head with oil; my cup overflows.*[250]

The word for "overflow" used in this passage is the Hebrew word רְוָיָה.
It is pronounced rev·ä·yä, and it simply means "to saturate, to run over." A wealthy, drunken overflow. When God fills your cup, you will overflow. We don't have to conjure or assemble anything; it simply says it will flow. It's not our job to produce the fruit and make it grow; it's merely our job to be a branch.

Do you remember this story from earlier?

> The one with the boy and his dad facing a log in the road?

The whole point was that he was powerless to do it himself; he needed his father to move the log with him. In this life, we are not at it alone.

The story is a poignant reminder of who accompanies us on our life's journey: the almighty God, the King of kings, the Lord of lords, the creator of all, and the all-powerful One. We need only let Him flow through us, allowing that truth to relieve the pressure we often place on ourselves.

> We are merely the microphone held up to God's mouth.

---

[250] Psalm 23:5.

> A microphone is never worried about what to say. Its only job is to amplify what's being spoken to it.[251]

Do you recall the scene of Jesus and the woman at the well? After a conversation with Jesus, the woman realizes His true identity and runs to share the news with her friends and family. What's incredible is that she doesn't have to perform miracles or work any magic—she simply overflows with her experience, and God takes care of the heavy lifting.

The Gospel of John recounts how she simply said to the people, "He told me everything I ever did." After meeting Jesus for themselves, they told the woman,

> We no longer believe just because of what you said; now we have heard for ourselves, and we know that this man really is the Savior of the world.[252]

I love this story because it reminds us that sometimes we get so caught up in saying the right things, quoting scripture flawlessly, and striving for perfection in leading people to Christ that we forget where the real power lies. It's not about convincing or persuading others that the table of faith is the best place to be; it's about sharing our own story and creating opportunities for others to experience Jesus for themselves.

---

[251] Hmm... Let that preach.
[252] John 4:42.

the table.

A wise woman once said, "If someone can talk you into something, someone else can talk you out of it."[253] So let's quit trying to persuade others and simply share our own journeys. Let's let God do the heavy lifting, because when people encounter the love and power of Jesus Christ themselves, everything changes. It's all about letting it happen—letting it overflow.

Let me close with this:

I spent a few months living in West Africa. I was stationed in a small, landlocked country called Burkina Faso. I stayed in a village filled with diverse African languages, and the idea of communicating my love for Jesus through words was impossible.

In spite of this, something extraordinary unfolded. I lived with a Muslim family, and there was a boy my age in the house. We quickly became close friends, bonding over work, soccer matches, and even hunting expeditions. We developed a friendship that transcended words. He knew I was there to visit Christian missionaries in the village, but he was a devout Muslim who made it clear he wouldn't be swayed.

I'll never forget his unwavering commitment to the Muslim Temple. Even in the midst of an intense soccer game, when prayer time arrived, he'd abruptly run off without a word to go to the temple. Initially, I was bewildered, but by the end of those months, it became an expected routine. Despite our differing faiths, soccer made us become close friends.

---

[253] Thanks, Beth. So true.

On my last day in Burkina Faso, we exchanged shirts as a symbol of our friendship and said our goodbyes with tears in our eyes. As I was on my fifteen-hour flight back home, I couldn't help but feel disappointed in my hopes that he would experience Jesus and begin to follow Him. In fact, he seemed even more devoted to Islam when I left than when I arrived.

However, two years later, I received a letter from my Muslim friend. The letter was in French, so I sought a friend's help to translate it into English. The moment he read it, my world turned upside down. It said, "Dear David, I hope you are doing well..." Then came the sentence that left me stunned: "I want you to know that I now walk with our Lord Jesus Christ. I want you to know that I have experienced His love and His power because of you."

I made the translator repeat that line multiple times, and I even double-checked with another translator to ensure it was real. It was an astonishing revelation. My Muslim brother had come to experience the love and power of Jesus Christ, and it had nothing to do with my words or marketing strategy—it was just the overflow of the Holy Spirit.

I have a phrase I repeat to myself often: "I can't mess up what God is doing." The scriptures tell us that one day, every knee will bow and every tongue will confess that Jesus is Lord. Everyone will eventually find their place at the table, and it's essential to remember that it's not all on us. Our role is simple: to sit, to overflow, and to go share our story. God takes care of the rest.

table talk

As a Christian, it doesn't matter what job you have or what you do in life—we're all supposed to reach out to others and share the teachings of Jesus. Whether you're a teacher, a business owner, a dog lover, a sports enthusiast, or even a mix of all these things, you've got a mission to help and tell others about Jesus. That's what the table is all about.

Consider this:

> Who in your circle are you called to share your story and invite to the table?

Prayer:

> God, help me out with _____. Grant me favor and wisdom as I interact with them. Lead us into organic conversations about you and your presence in my life.
>
> Amen.

you choose.

"Destiny is not a matter of chance; it is a matter of choice."
— William Jennings Bryan

"The choices you make in your life will make your life."
— Michael Josephson

"It is our choices, Harry, that show what we truly are, far more than our abilities."
— J.K. Rowling

Before we close this book, there's something we must address head-on.

Let's face it—life is not a cakewalk.

The reality is that there's always an enemy lurking, and it hates the table.

Just you even reading this book gives the enemy a headache.

Some of you may be reading this and might've spent years chasing God, praying your heart out, and feeling like He's playing hide and seek. You may have given it everything you've got, only to find your efforts seemingly fruitless.

In fact, many of you may have poured your heart and soul into the whole "church" or "religion" thing only to end up with a bunch of heartache and disappointment. It seems church trauma is a badge for most real Jesus followers.[254]

So, what's the reality?

The answer, though seemingly simple, carries profound weight:

> We have an enemy, a formidable adversary who despises nothing more than when people pull up a chair at the divine table.

But here is the other reality: Our God is greater.

Psalm 23 says something significant that, up until this moment, I've ignored.

> *He prepares a table before us...* <u>*in the presence of our enemies*</u>.[255]

> ....In the presence of our enemies.

We are literally sitting at this table with the enemy watching. The English word "presence" is translated from the

---

[254] Sad, but true. Especially with my millennial friends.
[255] Psalm 23:5.

Hebrew word נֶגֶד (new ·ghed). It literally means "in front of, face-to-face, before the eyes, in close proximity, awkwardly close."[256]

Psalm 23 is a beautiful poem and the theme passage of this book, but it doesn't shy away from acknowledging the bad guy. Here's the truth: We're invited to this incredible table, but our enemy is stalking nearby.

The Bible paints this foe as a fierce lion, prowling and looking for souls to devour.[257] Even when we're sitting at the table, he's right there—spewing threats, insults, and lies, telling us we don't belong, we're not good enough, and we've messed up.

And it has been at it for a long time, trying its best to pry you away with deceit—with lies.

Why does he do this? Because he can't stand it when we're in a close relationship with God. His goal is to distract us and to keep us from enjoying the blessings God has for us at the table.

The Chihuahua

I once found myself at a party, surrounded by delicious BBQ chicken that was about to be the highlight of my evening. However, my enjoyment was thwarted by a persistent, little troublemaker of a dog. This tiny creature was relentless, barking at me and scratching my shins and

---

[256] I'm willing to bet the devil has bad breath. He probably doesn't even brush his teeth.

[257] 1 Peter 5:8.

shoes. I wasn't really enjoying my time at that table until I purposefully turned my attention to the others at the table. I ignored the dog, and the dog walked away.

This is a lot like how our enemy operates.

Imagine our adversary as a pesky chihuahua consumed by jealousy. He craves you and your time and won't stop barking until he gets what he wants. Sometimes, we let it get to us. That dog distracts us, grabs our attention, and sometimes destroys our experience at the table.

Scripture lays it out:

> *For our struggle is not against flesh and blood, but against the rulers, against the authorities, against the powers of this dark world, and against the spiritual forces of evil in the heavenly realms.*[258]

In other words, our enemy isn't necessarily of human origin; when we sit at the table, we make some spiritual enemies. Sometimes, these rulers and authorities of the dark world resemble chihuahuas in the sense that they are annoying and unrelenting.[259] They pester us non-stop because these chihuahuas want your attention and hate the table.

It's easy to think that all we need to do is sit and enjoy the meal, but in reality, life will test us. Our relationship with God will be challenged. It's not always as easy and smooth

---

[258] Ephesians 6:12.

[259] I am not saying all chihuahuas are annoying. My grandma had one when I was a little kid that was pretty cute.

as we'd like it to be, but the feast is there, and we've been invited. So, let's dig in and face the chihuahuas of this world, trusting in the one who invited us.

    It's not like God doesn't see the enemy.

        God could have set the table anywhere he wanted.

            But no.

        There is intention. There is a meaning.

            It was purposeful when He set the table in front of the enemy.

This is a simple line that could have been left out, but let's be real. The enemy represents reality. Sitting at the table, experiencing God's abundance, and following Jesus all require laser focus and continual choice.
We have to continue to choose God every day. Especially when we are at the table, because that is where the dog barks the loudest.

But sometimes, choosing is difficult.

Choice

    Creating good habits is like making the right choice every time. When we fall out of routine, we fall out of the discipline of choice. With physical food, our bodies require us to eat regularly. If we miss a meal, our bodies remind us with physical hunger. However, in the spiritual realm, missing a spiritual meal can lead to a spiritual hunger—a hunger I'm afraid many of us have normalized.

Our bodies need a regular dose of spiritual food to keep us healthy, but we have to choose it. It's tricky, because if we miss a spiritual meal, the barking gets louder and it's easier to miss more. You've been there, right? You get into a healthy rhythm of church or prayer or reading the Bible, then you miss a day. It turns into a couple of days, and then you realize that it's been quite a while since you've "eaten."

I know I have taken breaks from some spiritual practices and have gone a while without spiritual nourishment without even noticing.

Some people will say they don't like reading the Bible or going to church, but here's the catch: The more you engage in these practices, the hungrier you become for spiritual growth. Reading the Bible, for instance, is like feasting on love letters from God, and it's a great foundation for a deeper spiritual life.

Don't believe the lies that say you can't be disciplined. Part of sticking to your spiritual practice is pushing through the slow days and even the days when you don't feel like it, just like staying healthy means hitting the gym and eating right even when you'd rather not. The whole premise of sitting at the table is eating the spiritual food your body and soul crave, so isn't it interesting that eating was also at the heart of the rejection of God and shame?

> *Now the serpent was more crafty than any of the wild animals the Lord God had made. He said to*

> the woman, "Did God really say, 'You must not eat from any tree in the garden'?"
> The woman said to the serpent, "We may eat fruit from the trees in the garden, but God did say, 'You must not eat fruit from the tree that is in the middle of the garden, and you must not touch it, or you will die.'"
> "You will not certainly die," the serpent said to the woman, "For God knows that when you eat from it, your eyes will be opened, and you will be like God, knowing good and evil."
> When the woman saw that the fruit of the tree was good for food and pleasing to the eye, and also desirable for gaining wisdom, she took some and ate it. She also gave some to her husband, who was with her, and he ate it.[260]

This is reality. This world is full of lying snakes and fruit that is pleasing to the eyes but bad for the spirit. God could have swooped in and saved Eve from making that choice, but he didn't.

> We have and will always have a choice.

I've always found it fascinating that in the garden of our ancestors, Adam and Eve, there were two types of trees: good trees and that one bad one. The good ones, God said we could freely eat from. I can imagine these trees were beautiful everywhere Adam and Eve looked. But right there,

---
[260] Genesis 3:1-6.

right in the middle of it all, as if it was staring them in the face, was that one tree—the one they were specifically told to avoid. It was right there, right in their faces. You know, "neh'·ghed," as they say. It's interesting how, even in the garden, they were in the presence of their enemy.

You'll encounter that one tree that's pleasing to the eye, the one you desire, the one that's seemingly in your face, and it can be incredibly hard to resist. Throughout history, men and women have fallen victim to this tree. Why? Because, in our human state, we're weak.

Many have fallen prey to what we've referred to as "the chihuahua." Now, in some ways, my analogy of the chihuahua isn't perfect. We often picture it as a scrawny dog with an annoying yelp, something we could easily kick aside, but this enemy is different. This enemy is strong, and unfortunately, when we're on our own, we're no match for it. In the book of 1 Peter, this chihuahua is described like this:

> ...Your enemy, the devil, prowls around like a roaring lion looking for someone to devour"[261]

This little chihuahua is strong, and as much as God desires for you to sit at the table, the roaring lion-chihuahua wants to devour you. And it (the devil) is exceptionally skilled at it. It's been going at it since the beginning of time and has become quite proficient. It knows our weaknesses. It knows what makes humans tick, and it has strategies that have

---

[261] 1 Peter 5:8.

been very successful in the history of the world. Frankly, on your own, you're just not strong enough.

We need an outside force, some accountability, some extra help. Scripture talks about this when it says,

> Be strong in the Lord and in His mighty power.[262]

In simple terms, it means, "Get your strength from the Lord." The first thing to realize is that in our own strength, we don't stand a chance against this enemy. This enemy is a formidable spiritual force that's directly against us and the table we want to sit at.

The devil—whether you call him Satan, Lucifer, a prowling lion, or even a chihuahua—knows that our connection to God and our source of strength is like a power outlet. It knows the table provides us with the five-course meal we need to be effective in this life. So, part of the enemy's strategy is to come between you and God, to wedge himself between you and your spiritual nourishment like a barrier at the dinner table.

When you're feeling overwhelmed, tempted, or pushed to walk away from that table, keep in mind the words of Jesus:
> My Father... is greater than all; no one can snatch you out of my Father's hand.[263]

This is a powerful idea because it says that nothing and no one can snatch you away from this table. The word

---

[262] Ephesians 6:10.
[263] John 10:29.

"snatch" is intentional; other translations use words like "pluck," "take," or even "pickpocket." These imply being stolen by surprise. The only way to leave the table is by your own choice.

There is our word again: choice.

I remember an old Sunday school song my grandma taught me as a child.
It goes like this:
> "This little light of mine, I'm gonna let it shine.
> This little light of mine, I'm gonna let it shine,
> let it shine, let it shine..."

There is a variation that goes, "I won't let Satan blow it out; I'm gonna let it shine."

There is so much truth to "letting" Satan blow out our light.
"Letting" has a whole lot to do with our "choice."
Satan is pretty good at trying to extinguish your light and tempt you away from the table. There's a Proverb that says, *Above all else, guard your heart.*[264]

"Guard" here isn't just a cute word; it's a military term, like a soldier headed into battle or a football player getting ready to tackle. Soldiers don't expect walking into the enemy's territory will be peaceful, and they don't expect the enemy to fight fair.

They are on guard.

> Get into your stance and protect yourself, because part of staying at the table is up to you.

---
[264] Proverbs 4:23.

Life will have its storms, unfortunate events, and challenges, but you need to be on guard. Sadly, the devil is skilled at convincing people to step away from the table. But the key is to not let him get to you; you've got to guard yourself.

What does it mean to guard yourself? Be smart. Be aware of your surroundings. Surround yourself with people who lift you up instead of bringing you down. Spend time in places that encourage you to stay at the table rather than luring you away.

Find some accountability.

I remember dealing with the same sexual curiosity any youthful boy had when I was young. Sex and sexuality is one of those things that is deeply beautiful that Satan has tried time and time again to pervert for so many. During my fight, I heard a man I deeply respected talk about his past struggles with sexual immorality. It made me realize I wasn't alone in dealing with this, and it encouraged me to talk about it and seek accountability.

Finding someone to talk to and keep yourself accountable makes going through a storm or taking a hit much easier. Going into battle with an army is a lot better than going alone.

But this part is on you.

Sitting at the table doesn't automatically come with friends and community; it's actually pretty easy to sit at a table, put your head down, and eat.

That's why we've been called to sit, *connect*, and share.

> In that order.
> It's one thing to
> sit, but we have to
> connect. We have
> to share.

Remember, God is with you, and He will see you through the struggles.

> *And the God of all grace, who called you to his eternal glory in Christ, after you have suffered a little while, will himself restore you and make you strong, firm, and steadfast. To him be the power forever and ever. Amen.*[265]

Notice that it doesn't say "if" you face tough times, but "when." When you encounter difficulties, God is there to personally mend your strength. Life can be challenging with the enemy constantly trying to pull you away from the table, but God offers the power and determination to remain seated. It's your choice to accept that assistance.

Help

The other day, I saw my four-year-old daughter struggling to open a string cheese. At first, she refused my help, saying, "No, I can do it." But eventually, with tears in her eyes, she brought the mangled cheese to me and said, "Daddy, can you help me?" I replied, "Of course, I was waiting for you to ask." I believe our heavenly Father is waiting for

---

[265] 1 Peter 5:10-11.

some of us to say the same thing: "I need your help." And I'm sure His response will be something like, "Absolutely, I was waiting for you to ask."

Once you sit at the table, it's like having insurance; it comes with protection. There's spiritual protection and support that comes with the chair, like a divine seatbelt. It doesn't guarantee you won't face challenges, but it does ensure you're safe from them.

As a matter of fact, you have already conquered them.

> *No, in all these things we are more than conquerors through him who loved us. For I am convinced that neither death nor life, neither angels nor demons, neither the present nor the future, nor any powers, neither height nor depth, nor anything else in all creation, will be able to separate us from the love of God that is in Christ Jesus our Lord.*[266]

Don't breeze past that sentence without noticing what you are called: more than a conqueror. You, my friend, are not only a conqueror; you are more than a conqueror. What is that?[267] I really don't know, but I know it means you win.

Imagine going into battle and facing challenges that you already know you have won and have conquered. I wonder how many battles you have seen in your life. I wonder how many you have walked through, confident in victory. I wonder how many times the enemy has tried to rip you from your

---

[266] Romans 8:37-39.
[267] It's more...?

God-given seat at the table. I wonder how many times you let him win. I want to pause here for a moment because some of you, my friends, have messed up. Scratch that, *all* of us have messed up.[268]

The chihuahua, as I like to call it, sometimes gets the better of us, and that's okay. It's normal. It's human. The Bible says that we have all fallen short of the glory of God.[269] In other words, in our best efforts, we are still imperfect. My kids, at our family dinner table at home, have spilled their milk, gotten up out of their seat, dropped their plate, fussed, and done this and that. I once even caught my daughter drawing on our recently painted wall with a pen. This type of behavior is usually followed with a little reprimand. Usually, a simple look for my kids lets them know that they are in the wrong. But sometimes it gets to a point where they want to leave the table. I hurt their feelings and they run to their room. But the thing is, I have always invited them back. Just because they have messed up once or twice or five-hundred times doesn't mean they are not part of the family. It doesn't mean they have to eat outside. It simply means we have some things to work on. In the same way, we (you and I) have some junk to work on. It doesn't make God hate you, and it doesn't mean you have to leave the table; it just means we are a work in progress—like a beautiful painting that the painter will not quit on until he has it just the way he wants it. God will not leave you. I heard a quote once, I believe it was Max

---

[268] When I was writing that line, it was about nine in the morning. I had already messed up four times that day. More to come, guaranteed.

[269] Romans 3:23.

Lucado who said, "God loves you just the way you are, but He loves you too much to leave you that way." You are a work in progress, and that should take some of the pressure off of you.

You are sons and daughters of the King.
>	You are princes and princesses.
>>	You always have a seat at the royal table.
>>>	There is nothing you could do to have
>>>	God take your nameplate off that chair.
>>>	You are His.
>>>>	You are loved and wanted.

My kids, Daisy and Jack, could never, ever do anything that would make them not part of my family. They could cuss me out, they could tell me I am terrible, they could wreck my car, they could spit out my food, heck, they could even tell me I wasn't their dad anymore. But the truth is, they will always be my children. My love for them will never go away, and they will always have a seat at my table.

Sons and daughters of the King, you are seen,
>	you are chosen,
>>	you are enough,
>>>	you are worthy,
>>>>	you are adopted,
>>>>>	and you have been invited to
>>>>>	live the abundant life in our Lord
>>>>>	Jesus' name.

But we must remember that this annoying, barking enemy does not want you to know that. He wins if he can get a little shame or lack of confidence in your head. That devil doesn't want you to know that he was defeated by Jesus and the cross. He doesn't want you to remember that our Daddy is bigger and stronger than he is. He doesn't want you to learn that this match has already been decided.
It's already been won.
We are not fighting for our victory; we are fighting from His victory.

> We live in the greatest era of human history: post-resurrection. Which means the war is over.
>> Evil has zero power over Jesus and, in the same way, it has zero power over you.

Steer Clear

Sometimes I ride my bike to work, and there's this house that I pass on the way with a bunch of dogs. Behind their fence, they bark up a storm. I know they can't reach me no matter how ferociously they bark, so I keep on riding. In fact, when I am near that house, I often switch to the other side of the road to escape the noise. Sometimes, I even take a different route just to avoid it. This canine chorus, oddly enough, mirrors life's challenges. The devil, much like those dogs, can't harm you because you're protected by the Holy Spirit's power.

But you can still choose to steer clear of certain places.

It's called wisdom and discernment.

There's a saying I've heard that goes, "If you want to lose weight, stay out of the bakery." In essence, it means that if you aim to lead a good life and you're weary of hearing the devil's lies and threats, then avoid situations that cause them to worsen. Keep a healthy distance between you and the devil. As Saint James says, "Resist the devil, and he will flee from you."[270] You do this by sidestepping things that drag you down spiritually. Loitering around the bakery is like flirting with disobedience; it gives the devil an opportunity to attack and influence you. It's like pitching a tent right next to the barking dog. As a believer, you certainly have the strength to endure without getting bitten by the dog, but why dwell there? Eventually, we break under the relentless annoyance.

You see, hearing constant lies makes it easy to believe one eventually, just like how playing with fire leads to getting burned. Engaging in things you shouldn't gives the evil one a foothold in your life. Scripture reminds us not to provide the devil anything—not even a foothold.[271]

You won't win this spiritual battle alone, just like I can't outrun the dogs unless there's a fence and some soon-to-be help. Success comes when you draw your strength from the ultimate power source—God Himself.

So, remember to resist the devil while standing firm in your faith. You're not alone in your struggles; the family of believers worldwide is going through similar challenges. The

---

[270] James 4:7.
[271] Ephesians 4:27. Think of a foothold like in rock climbing. Without one, you can't climb.

God of all grace, who has called you to His eternal glory in Christ, will personally restore and strengthen you after a bit of suffering. To Him belongs the power forever and ever.[272]

I love how the scriptures emphasize staying vigilant and withstanding attack, but they are also filled with reminders of God's power and strength. In Him, you'll discover the fortitude to "stand firm against the strategies of the devil." The devil has meticulously planned ways to attack, but here's the twist—he loses, and God reigns supreme.

You Are No Slave

On September 22, 1862, Abraham Lincoln signed the Emancipation Proclamation, which declared freedom for all slaves across the United States. Though sadly, in the Southern areas of the United States, nothing really changed. Freed African-Americans were still living as if they were in chains, obedient to their former masters. Why? Because they didn't know how to break free, or (possibly) they lacked the courage and means to do so.

You, my friend, need not walk through life in chains. Acknowledge who you are and the freedom you've been granted. Be courageous, claim your liberty, and walk and live in that freedom. You have the power of the Holy Spirit within you. The devil doesn't stand a chance against you.

It's not your name that matters; it's what you answer to. There's a story where Jesus confronts a man enslaved by evil spirits. No one could contain him; he was like a wild man

---

[272] 1 Peter 5:9-11, summarized.

living among the tombs. When Jesus approached, the man fell before Him, pleading not to be tortured. Jesus asked him his name, and the man replied, "Legion, for we are many." This poor soul had been labeled "Legion" for so long that he had forgotten his true identity. It's time to shake off those false labels and remember your real name. You might have been enslaved for a while, but that's not your identity. Your name is written in the book of the King—you're a child of the divine. Don't answer to what the world has labeled you. Know your name, even when the enemy tries to make you forget. You're free, and the devil doesn't stand a chance.

> Don't be duped by the deceiver.
> Don't be fooled by the father of lies.
> Live in the truth of our triumphant God.

Read the words of Jesus:

> *In this world you will have trouble. But take heart! I have overcome the world.*[273]

---
[273] John 13:33.

The title of this chapter is "you choose."
It seems so simple,
but it's not; it's a battle.
There will be trouble,
but take heart; He's won.

Choose to win.

table talk

Stand up tall.

Take a deep breath.
God's got this. Even this.

Whatever you are walking through right now, The Lord is by your side. And you are exactly where you are supposed to be. Do you believe that? Reflect on your current circumstances.

God is in the character-building business, and He will use the circumstances of life to continue making you who you need to be.

Let me say it again: You are exactly where He wants you.

You have the power. Power over that addiction, that depression, and that enemy. Lean into the power promised in the Holy Spirit.

Pray a prayer of protection and deliverance over yourself and those you care about.

Spend a moment and meditate on Psalm 18.
End with a prayer thanking God.

closing

My parents had a tiny plastic table with little plastic chairs.
The top was a yellowish-white, and the legs were blue;
        a blue that only lived in the eighties.

I reached for my milk and my elbow tapped my glass.

        The Father looked at me and
        smiled. He cleaned up my mess and
        continued the conversation.

            Feelings of shame and guilt
            are absent at this table.

        I am convinced of this table.
                God's table.

            It takes us however we are to
            make us who we are supposed
            to be.

    To live an abundant life
        full of God's grace, love, and power.

You are invited to the table—to eat, connect, and overflow.

I have always thought that some of the vintage Disney movie endings were cheesy when they said, "...and they lived happily ever after," but I believe that is what the house of the Lord is like. There will be storms, there will be wind and rain, and there will be barking chihuahuas. It's not going to be easy, but know this:

> The Lord is your shepherd and you lack nothing. He gives you rest in peaceful green pastures
> next to a quiet stream.
> He refreshes you.

> He guides you down the right and perfect paths of life. Even though there will be darkness and hurt,
> you will not be afraid
> because He is with you.
> Even now, the Shepherd is with you.

> His strength gives you peace and comfort.

> He has invited you to the table to feast and live with your friends and family.

> Even though the enemy is still around,
> he can't touch you.

The Holy Spirit is upon you; you have been anointed and will overflow with love, joy, peace, forbearance, kindness, goodness, faithfulness, gentleness, and self-control.

This will be with you forever, all the days of your life.
This table is home.
Forever.
And so you live happily ever after, along with your family and friends.

Come, sit at the table
and eat.
Believe me, it's good.

My friend, spending time with you at this table has been an honor. Please, read and receive this blessing:

    Father, Jesus, and Holy Spirit,
        I declare the promise
        of Your abundant life
        over the reader of
        this prayer.

        May they find their seat
        at Your table.
        May they taste
        and see that You
        are good.
            And may You,
        Lord, overflow
        into every area of
        their life.
            Right now.

        In the glorious, powerful,
        and matchless name of
        Jesus Christ.
            amen

special thanks

I couldn't have embarked on this journey without a little help and a whole lot of heart. Here's a shout-out to those who made this adventure all the more exciting:

My wife – For being my rock, my cheerleader, and my constant source of unconditional support. You're my favorite teammate, and I'm eternally grateful for all that you do.

David Hawes, Casey Hawes, and David Obwald – You three were the wind beneath my writing wings, and your encouragement and nudges to publish meant the world to me. Thank you for not letting me off the hook.

Henry and Megan, Rob and Jessica, Nathan and Nicole – Thanks for actually sitting around a table with me and diving into the depths of this book. You made this journey not only collaborative, but also incredibly memorable.

Pastor David, Pastor Steve, and Pastor Karl – These spiritual sheriffs ensured I didn't stray too far from the theological path. Thanks for keeping my writing on the righteous road!

Richard and my friends at Genesis Publishing House –
Thank you for your expertise and unwavering support—
even when I was a bit of an irritant 😊

Vaviana – Thank you for your skills and belief in me.
You truly helped me cross the finish line.

And to everyone who played a part
in this book's creation:
it wouldn't be the same without
you. Here's to the next
adventure and the many more
stories yet to come! –DW

www.ingramcontent.com/pod-product-compliance
Lightning Source LLC
Chambersburg PA
CBHW031523040125
19925CB00012B/603